Learning and the Professors

LEARNING
AND THE
PROFESSORS

Edited by

OHMER MILTON
Learning Resources Center
The University of Tennessee

and

EDWARD JOSEPH SHOBEN, JR.
Commission on Academic Affairs
American Council on Education

OHIO UNIVERSITY PRESS, Athens, Ohio

CONTRIBUTORS

Paul L. Dressel, Director of Institutional Research
Michigan State University

Ruth E. Eckert, Professor of Higher Education
University of Minnesota

John W. Gardner, Former Secretary
Department of Health, Education, and Welfare

Howard Gruber, Professor, Institute for Cognitive Studies
Rutgers University

Donald P. Hoyt, Coordinator of Research Services
American College Testing Program

William R. Hutchison, Professor of History and American Studies
American University

Henry C. Johnson, Jr., Assistant Professor of Education
Illinois State University

Irvin J. Lehmann, Associate Professor
Michigan State University

Ross L. Mooney, Professor of Education
Ohio State University

Daniel C. Neale, Associate Professor of Educational Psychology
University of Minnesota

C. Robert Pace, Professor of Higher Education
University of California

Sidney L. Pressey, Professor Emeritus
Ohio State University

Laurence Siegel, Chairman, Department of Psychology
Louisiana State University

Logan Wilson, President
American Council on Education

FOREWORD

Most exhortative literature is like shooting into the air. It may flare brilliantly but briefly, and if it frightens the surprised observer, he will often walk away muttering but untouched. Since such literature is usually directed to getting people's attention, it often lacks the concentration which is needed to produce the corrective action desired by the exhorter-critic. The general public, so often barraged by sharp warnings of societal problems, may feel uneasy about a new outburst but also helpless. Since no specific group is asked to assume specific responsibilities, none do.

The editors of *Learning and the Professors* have not followed the pattern of most exhortative literature. While Ohmer Milton and Edward Joseph Shoben, Jr. believe that a number of "the intractable realities demand a reappraisal of instructional practices in our colleges and universities," they have not been content to expose these realities to general scrutiny. They have addressed their book specifically to the people they believe are capable of making the reappraisal and taking the necessary remedial action. Milton and Shoben believe that the faculty are "in direct control of many of the conditions for learning" and individually and of their own initiative could alter and improve the quality of instruction. Moreover, as a collectivity, the faculty, through the educational policies it adopts, the curricula it revises, and the practices it perpetuates, partially shapes what takes place in the classrooms of others and what transpires outside the classroom. The very title of the present collection of articles implies the active, causal role of the professor deliberately intervening in and controlling much of the learning process of the student. A second, more subtle meaning of the title, also appropriate to the volume, is that the learning process of the professor himself must be continuous. The dual linkage of learning and the professor, one hopes, may recall Chaucer's clerk, of whom it was said, "gladly wolde he lerne, and gladly teche."

Obviously, he who would be instrumental in guiding others to learn must be deeply immersed in learning himself. What the editors ask through their selection of articles and their introductory and concluding chapters is that the faculty member have a high enthusiasm and concern not only for what he is teaching but also for how he teaches. Just as it is the business of the faculty member to keep abreast of or lead the search for new knowledge in his own field of, say, French literature or theoretical biology, it is equally his business to probe the efficacy of the lecture system, the grading system, the campus environment, the academic timetable, and, indeed, all the practices and assumptions that have become barnacled to institutions of higher learning. Most of all, he must become self-conscious, aware of the implications of what he does and its impact on the educational process itself.

Each reprinted article, therefore, has been chosen to help educators, in Shoben's tactful resurrection of Lincoln's phrase, "disenthrall" themselves from the academic *status quo*. Thus, there is a provocative skepticism about the practices of formal higher education, an asking of whether there is not a limit to the value of such formal education, whether some of it could not be performed off the campus, whether the years spent in such education could not be shortened. The authors point to the lack of correlation between collegiate classroom success and career success; they cite research findings in which students who do not attend lectures do as well or better than students who do. They dispel the myth of "publish or perish"—Logan Wilson for example, says that "in all except a few leading institutions less than 10 per cent of the faculty accounts for 90 per cent or more of all published research"—and they find that those who oppose educational television are more anxious and more authoritarian than those who favor it. With an aura of healthy irreverence towards traditional attitudes and customs, the authors make a number of interesting suggestions: for example, to abandon the freshman year (let students pass tests to get into higher division classes at their own speed), to reduce the needless publication strain on teachers, to curtail the lecture course, replacing it with seminars, directed independent study, and occasional lectures on unpublished work.

Not all of *Learning and the Professors* is full of cheerful possibilities for the future campus. The sobering factor, as implied by the volume, is not the numbers and character of the new student body, not the rapid change of society, the rising costs of education, the burgeoning of scientific knowledge, the competitive attractions of politics or recreation or service or money-making in the world outside the campus. All of these compelling conditions could be coped with, the editors suggest, if only faculties were willing to study, evaluate, and then change their ways. But the editors are far from sanguine that faculties will accept such self-analysis, self-surgery, and self-reconstruction. From the first chapter, we are reminded that faculties are conservative: It was teachers, not students, who resisted the introduction of books on early American campuses. And, at the last chapter, we are confirmed in the view that faculty find their greatest rewards in activities where their relationship to students is most tenuous. The only chapter on institutional change, that by Professor Mooney, describes how difficult, how nearly impossible, it is to move towards integral, developmental goals because power at universities is so fragmented, and what power there is is generally put to negative use, nullifying the efforts of someone else.

Learning and the Professors, then, is both stimulating and sobering, both imaginative and realistic. One of its greatest values may come from making the academic person more capable of realizing the powers he does possess, by helping him to develop his potentialities for self-awareness. Academics have always been self-conscious, distinguishing themselves from the general community in dress, style of life, habitual preoccupations and prerogatives, particularly those relating to freedom of speech. But they have not always been self-conscious by being self-analytic or self-critical in their instructional or institutional roles. They have not been living "the examined life" in either the social scientific sense or the Socratic one—or even the

Freudian one. Whether they can, is the question. The editors of *Learning and the Professors* will have done a profound service for all of us engaged in education if they succeed in prodding some of us to "disenthrall" ourselves and truly examine our lives.

MARTIN MEYERSON
President, SUNY-Buffalo
Member, Commission on Academic
    Affairs, American Council
    on Education

PREFACE

At least four intractable realities demand a reappraisal of instructional practices in our colleges and universities. One is the huge leap in enrollments. A second is the burgeoning of knowledge. A third is the new opportunities for faculty members to engage in significant research and advisory roles. Finally, there is the radical character of social change which makes the sheer transmission of the cultural heritage a necessary but no longer sufficient preparation for citizenship in the world of tomorrow. Because of these factors, this little book is dedicated to the stimulation of informed and disciplined thought, followed by responsible and imaginative action, about instructional issues. The proper leaders here, in our eyes, are the professors themselves.

There were literally thousands of articles from which to select those for this book. Several guiding principles determined final choices. First, there are those selections which challenge the *status quo* in American higher education. Second, there are those which suggest novel programs and procedures that stem from research-based knowledge. These selections also point toward additional cogent research. Third, in most of the articles, the technical jargon of statisticians and social science investigators is at a minimum. Fourth, the pieces were chosen for their intellectual quality and professional relevance. Finally, these articles are not intended to be representative of the vast literature of higher education; rather, they reflect the considered views (sometimes villainously styled the "prejudices") of the editors.

We wish to acknowledge the courtesy of the authors and publishers who gave permission to include their material in this volume. Specific recognition is made on pages 215–16. Special thanks go to Mrs. Barbara Wickersham of the Learning Resources Center of The University of Tennessee for her secretarial skills and for the humane adroitness and good humor with which she guided two busy men toward the completion of this book.

O.M.
E.J.S.

January, 1968

CONTENTS

INTRODUCTION

This little book is based on four hopes which its editors regard as desperately crucial if contemporary higher education is to serve effectively the nation and the nation's youth. Those hopes are (1) that there is a degree of receptivity among today's professors to information and fact-disciplined ideas about the substantial changes that are necessary in our educative ways of dealing with students, (2) that recent thought and investigation concerning the optimum arrangements for teaching and learning can be critically but rapidly assimilated into the cultures of our colleges, (3) that faculties can play key parts in using systematic knowledge to make their own campuses more productive environments for humanly significant learning, and (4) that the enterprise of improving the teaching-learning process is properly understood as sufficiently complex and important to command the intellect and imagination of the professoriate.

None of these hopes can be readily realized. Knowledge about the issues underlying each of them is fragmented, elusive, and subject to the influences of many kinds of variables not easy to control or even to recognize. This state of affairs, however, is a familiar one among the intellectually disposed, and the first steps in attacking such realms of significant ambiguity are the customary ones of tough-minded reflection, penetrating discussion, and informed debate on the grand scale within the scholarly community. If this little anthology rests on the grandiose vision of markedly superior education in our colleges and universities, it also recognizes that its first job is to provide some assistance to faculties in reconsidering the deeply entrenched patterns of instruction and curricular offerings that obtain on the great majority of our campuses. Any *status quo* is usually an object of critical concern among the restless heads who view the world from above professorial gowns; the question here is one of whether these same critical minds can direct themselves creatively to their own central task of furthering the scope and effectiveness of learning for *all* members of the academic community, especially those members called students.

As is well known, our growing colleges and universities are so structured as to promote distance and isolation among the members of the various subject-matter disciplines. Issues and problems in the teaching-learning venture which cut across conventional departmental boundaries are, therefore, hard to bring into focus as common concerns; and because they do not "belong" to a particular discipline, they are seldom perceived as relevant for professors whose identities are conceived as tightly bound to disciplinary membership. The evaluation of student achievement is a ready case in point. How much sophistication about so touchy and crucial a matter as grading is available, widely shared, and used as a basis for policy on any given campus? That many faculty members have thought about such matters extensively and in depth there is little doubt; but for the most part, their reflections have rarely become part of the common concerns that animate and define the character of an institution of higher learning. Indeed, there is something sadly typical about the reaction of several relatively senior and not undistinguished professors who, helping recently to plan a research project on instruction at one of our large universities, remarked that the group's discussion of instructional problems was the first in which they had participated during their considerable careers as teachers.

In consequence, acting on our hopes, we feel impelled to propose that this collection of recent provocative articles (some of them original to the volume) be used as a base or a common point of departure for a variety of meetings and seminars among faculties—and not infrequently with student participants—toward the end of improving our arrangements for learning and teaching in American higher education. We are firmly convinced that eventual solutions are most likely to arise from vigorous and continued exchanges of ideas and insights from across the several disciplines and from among the several constituencies of a given institution.

Each college or university must, by its own processes, decide for itself how to create the climate within which such reflective but action-oriented discussions can take root and thrive. Something can be learned, we think, from the models of the teach-ins that grew up around the issues of civil rights and foreign policy. Few professors or administrators currently need strong reminders that "educational reform" presently carries for large numbers of informed and vocal students some of the same energy and concern as voter registration or our problems in southeast Asia. The patient but persistent cultivation of faculty luncheon groups has shown profitable payoffs in some institutions. Seminars on the relationship of teaching to learning, following in some respects the highly successful University Seminars that Frank Tannenbaum instituted at Columbia, can demonstrate the intellectual respectability and the humane significance of the matters discussed here. Occasional convocations, especially with participants from other campuses, are useful if buttressed by ongoing efforts at home; and a strongly conceived program for the in-service development of faculty members as teachers may be the most relevant and most productive of all. When William James indicated that the first lecture he heard in psychology was the first he gave, he was uttering no boast, and his remark leaves room to wonder how many students have been seriously handicapped by the lack of preparation for the professorial role afforded lesser men than James.

Here lies the central problem: College teaching is probably the only profession in the world for which no specific training is required. The profession of scholarship is rich in prerequisites for entry, but not that of instruction. In the face of the straightforwardly educational demands now being levied as never before on our colleges and universities, how can we correct this historic—and anachronistic—state of affairs that "bugs" so many of our swelling numbers of students? *Learning and the Professors* is humbly submitted as one small step toward a decent, effective, and intellectually exciting resolution of that great difficulty.

OHMER MILTON
EDWARD JOSEPH SHOBEN, JR.

1

THE STATE OF THE ESTABLISHMENT

Ohmer Milton

Ohmer Milton, Professor of Psychology and Director of the Learning
Resources Center, The University of Tennessee, has conducted exten-
sive investigations of college instruction during the past ten years.
His books include *Behavior Disorders: Perspectives and Trends* and
Effective College Learning.

Teaching-learning arrangements have been taken for
granted, for the most part, throughout the history of higher
education; the instructional procedures and approaches of today
are much the same as those of yesteryear. Such practices and
conditions for learning as frequency of class meetings, the fifty-
minute hour, lecturing, course loads, credits, grading, advising,
rigid degree requirements, demand for small classes, and many
others seem to be accepted by the vast majority of faculty
members as established and enduring "truths" for effective and
efficient undergraduate instruction. Yet a college or university is
a complex environment which exists for the primary purpose of
promoting increasingly diverse and varied learning—from the
simple to the complex, from the concrete to the abstract, from
the mundane to the ethereal, and from the past into the future.

Judging, too, by the rigidity and inflexibility of teaching-
learning practices on a given campus, as well as by the similarity
of them from campus to campus (there are rare notable exceptions), there has even been denial of the diversities. Courses
ranging from Elementary Anthropology to Advanced Zoology
fit into almost identical academic routines. Differences among
students have been denied to a marked degree in that, generally

speaking, all of them have been expected or required to progress at the same pace through a four-year academic regime. The brilliant student and the much less than brilliant one lock-step together.

CHALLENGING "TRUTHS"

Of all the "truths," the most enduring and tenacious one is that of the *necessity* of personal contact between professor and student. Somehow a mysterious or magic force develops as a function of the association which promotes learning and achievement—or so goes the belief; if the force is absent, as perforce it must be in such arrangements for learning as large classes or television presentations, there can be *no* learning. Catalogues and other college publications perpetuate this "truth" by proclaiming low student-teacher ratios; presumably the nearer the ratio approaches one to one, the better the teaching-learning process is deemed to advance. (Incidentally, classes are supposed to become smaller and smaller as one goes *up* the educational ladder from the first grade through graduate school; evidently, adults are more influenced by the "mysterious force" than are young children.) Much current recruiting propaganda conveys a similar theme. For example, a *large* university beams to high school seniors: "Each faculty member has been selected not only on the basis of his scholarly attainment but also because of his active interest in the educational development and day to day problems of young people."

Thus, the current panacea offered by educators for whatever difficulties colleges are having with students is a return to small classes. It is interesting to note that the "small class notion" originated many *centuries* ago:

> Historically, where did we get our fixed notion of one teacher for every 25 students? I have searched long. With a clue from a casual conversation and with the aid of an eminent Talmudic scholar, President Samuel Belkin of Yeshiva University, I now find the answer goes back to at least the middle of the 3rd century. In Babylonian Talmud Baba Bathra 21A the rule was established by Rabbi Raba, an authoritative sage of his era: "25 students are to be

enrolled in one class. If there are from 25 to 40 an assistant must be obtained. Above 40, two teachers are to be engaged." [1]

At the same time, it is axiomatic (a) that all classes for all courses should continue to meet on a similar and regular basis, (b) that "teaching" is primarily the dispensing of knowledge via talking, (c) that grades are good indicators of success in other endeavors, (d) that students are eager to learn those things a college wishes them to learn, and (e) that increasing fractionation of subject matter promotes intellectual acumen by undergraduates.

On the other hand, quite different attitudes from those toward the "truths" of teaching prevail toward "truths" in our own domains of scholarship. Such "truths" in academic specialties are perpetual targets for penetrating inquiry. To those ends we even *seek* criticisms of our research efforts; this stems from the recognition that genuine truths are elusive and that there are individual limitations in pursuing them. Within this context, the fact that the "truths" of college instruction have not been questioned on a grand scale appears singularly incongruent.

As scholars and scientists, then, how can we allow teaching-learning "truths" to go unchallenged? Surely, for example, something other than a mysterious or magic force operates when there is personal contact between professor and student; surely there are elements or characteristics of this personal contact which can be identified; surely personal contact operates differentially from student to student; surely personal contact varies in significance among the academic specialties. If these assertions are true, personal contact can be exploited—beneficially for students—to a far greater extent than appears to be the case today. Small classes may not always be the most effective vehicle or structure for its operation!

If, on the other hand, the personal contact notion proves to be less powerful than it is believed to be, then continual emphasis upon it, especially by implication and innuendo, is both misleading and unfair to college students. Might not the development of the crucial realization that learning, in the final analysis, is an individual and personal matter, be unfortunately delayed?

FOUNDATIONS FOR CHANGE

There are at least two compelling sets of circumstances to support the proposition that most of the current and traditional conditions for learning can no longer be accepted with complacency:

(1) Most of the present arrangements for learning originated at a time when only a small select portion of the population was in college; today the student body is heterogeneous in many respects. Around 1900, approximately four per cent of young people in the 18–22 age group were in college; today, approximately 48 per cent of that group attend institutions of higher learning; the percentage is expected to reach 60 within a few years. Moreover, there was much less "knowledge" then than there is now.

(2) There is the reality of sheer numbers. Between six and seven million undergraduates at the present time and additional millions within the next few years cannot be instructed in the same fashion as a few thousand were a century or two ago. This fact of sheer numbers of students is complicated by the fact of shortages of faculty members in selected fields; for example, in chemistry, physics, and psychology, only 22.8 per cent, 28.7 per cent, and 37.2 per cent, respectively, of graduates obtaining doctor's degrees in the years 1962–63 and 1963–64 entered college teaching.[2]

Furthermore, a basic question for our nation is this one: Are we proceeding within our colleges and universities in such a fashion that there will be maximum benefits for the young people who come to us? There is some evidence to suggest that the answer is "No" for many students. The selections in this book contain some of the evidence; other evidence is to be found in magazine articles and newspaper reports of student behavior that ranges from uncontrolled explosiveness to apathy.

Certainly, however, more definitive answers to this question and an effective resolution of the issue of soaring enrollments entail far more than teaching-learning arrangements and encompass far greater territory than that of college campuses. Nevertheless, faculty members are in *direct control* of many of the conditions for learning; they are in a position to alter them in many dimensions and directions. On many campuses, they not only control activities within their own classrooms, but they also determine, to a large extent, the academic policies and procedures which guide their institutions.

Until recently, there has been little need for faculty members to concern themselves with the sorts of teaching-learning issues posed in this book. Students were relatively few in number and faculty members were relatively plentiful. With this situation reversed and the temper of the times radically altered, there seems to be a marked resistance on the part of many college teachers to broadening their responsibilities beyond the mere presentation of content or to facing the necessity for thoughtfully modifying their teaching roles.

In this regard, the literature has little to offer about faculty members and the "whys" of their behavior. Whereas much is known about students, little is known about faculties. One investigation,[3] however, directed toward exploring the attitudes and values of professors (the possible use of educational television was the focal point), offers a few most enlightening cues. Eighty per cent of a faculty of 400 responded via questionnaires, and two selected groups of them were studied via "depth" interviews.

Eighty-five per cent of the responding group believed that they were "good" teachers. As for issues in teaching-learning, the majority felt that emphasis upon subject-matter content was far more important than all other aspects of instruction. Lecturing was, without question, the most frequently utilized and preferred approach in teaching. One of the most interesting findings for members of the entire group was a tendency for them to score toward the authoritarian pole on a scale designed to measure equalitarian-authoritarian attitudes.

Striking "personality" differences were found between two

extreme groups—those who were very much in favor of instructional television and those who strongly opposed it. Those in the former category, in contrast to those in the latter, tended to be more tolerant people, to possess a greater tolerance for change, and to be more willing to use a greater variety of approaches in both teaching and evaluation. The pro-TV professor was found most often to be a member of a department where his general views were opposed by his colleagues, suggesting considerable strength in maintaining his own values as an individual.

Members of the anti-TV group expressed fears of job loss, concern about the creation of a "star" system, and anxiety about the possibility of their exposure through television to criticism by their colleagues. The anti-TV professor tended to be a member of a department wherein his anti-TV views were shared by his colleagues.

Frederick Rudolph has documented the fact that during the early days of colleges in the United States, faculties were slow in beginning to use *books*. Student literary societies welcomed books on campuses and hastened a place for them in the educational enterprise at a time when piety was the chief concern of those in charge.[4] (One interpretation of the continuing emphasis upon lecturing is that there still exists a reluctance to admit the value of books for student learning.)

SYSTEMATIC KNOWLEDGE

Some knowledgeable individuals believe that major changes in teaching-learning arrangements are now inevitable. These alterations may occur primarily in publicly supported institutions, because they are the ones in which the great majority of students will continue to be enrolled.

Assuming that alterations are forthcoming, it appears that there are two choices—emergency measures *or* measures based upon systematic knowledge. The former are seldom effective for solving any problems and in many instances make them worse. Television teaching may already be in this category; on many campuses, it is a way of perpetuating the maxim that "teaching is talking." Utilization of measures and approaches, on the other hand, that are based upon systematic knowledge ideally represents the very essence of the university enterprise.

Perhaps the best illustrations of pervasive procedures which are *not* based upon systematic knowledge are those of evaluation of student achievement and the decisions to which the measures lead. It has been *assumed* throughout the years that grades and grade-point averages reflect not only academic accomplishment but that they also serve as good indicators of future non-academic attainments; consequently, they continue to be used as a major basis for many important decisions about students—honors, financial aid, campus leadership positions, job choices, graduate school entry, and others.

Yet during the past few years, revealing and sobering studies have shown: (a) extreme variations in grading practices within and among faculties in various institutions, (b) tenuous and highly suspect relationships between grades and nonacademic endeavors, (c) percentages of unsatisfactory grades remaining constant or even increasing as ability levels of student bodies show an upward trend, and (d) many untoward impacts of evaluation upon students.

Brief mention of only two investigations may provide some substantiating evidence for these assertions. J. A. Davis of the National Opinion Research Center surveyed 1,673 seniors from 135 colleges and universities; all had been National Merit Scholarship holders, finalists, or semifinalists. Seventy per cent of these students of outstanding academic aptitude had received top grades in the lowest quality schools; only 36 per cent of them received comparable grades in the highest quality ones. Many of these superior young people with *less than a B+ average* in the high-ranking schools chose *not* to pursue graduate study; they underestimated their academic abilities. Their self-esteem and their aspirations were lowered because the faculties had judged them solely on the basis of personal and local standards.[5] Thistlethwaite of Vanderbilt University obtained similar results in a survey of 2,000 students from 140 institutions.[6]

A central thesis of *The American College*, perhaps the most

comprehensive single document available about higher education, is: "The scientific method, more than any other procedure
known to man, provides the basis for intelligent change: change
based on systematic knowledge rather than on improvisation,
hunch, or dogma." [7]

This is to say that the spirit or essence of the scientific method
is that of seeking sound evidence to support positions in place of
"hunch" or "dogma" or mere tradition. Many routes to knowledge, varying from field to field, all have in common the quest
for broader and deeper perceptions of reality and the reduction
of illusion. For scores of years, higher education has made many
unsubstantiated claims about cause-effect relationships in student achievement. Sound evidence is now available that raises
serious doubts about the validity of many of the assertions.
Needless to say, further evidence about teaching-learning issues
is necessary and should be sought. Higher education as an
institution should be the last to make unsubstantiated claims
about the determinants of student attainments.

For all the foregoing reasons, all faculty members as well as
prospective ones need to:

(1) become aware of fact-disciplined ideas from a multitude
    of sources which indicate that changes are necessary in
    our ways of dealing with students;

(2) become acquainted with recent thinking, grounded in
    systematic knowledge, about potentially more effective
    teaching-learning arrangements;

(3) seek modifications, based upon sound evidence, in the
    teaching-learning arrangements obtaining on their own
    campuses; and

(4) redouble their efforts to identify crucial variables in the
    teaching-learning process.

FUNDAMENTAL QUESTIONS

Are we proceeding within our colleges and universities in
such a fashion that there will be maximum benefits for our
students? In considering this basic problem, the thoughtful
reader may find useful guides to his own reflections in the
following sorts of questions:

(1) In view of the availability of a vast array of devices for dispensing information—television, programmed materials, tape recorders, and inexpensive and widely available *books*—what is the most educationally appropriate and distinctive future role of the professor in the college classroom?

(2) What are some of our practices which should be altered so as to place greater responsibility upon the student for his own learning?

(3) Should the role of the faculty continue to be essentially the same in both freshman and senior courses?

(4) What is the evidence to support our claims that students gain, for example, in ability to think critically and to respect honest differences of opinion? What contributions do we really make in the development of those characteristics?

(5) Do many of our practices with undergraduates merely prolong adolescence?

(6) In view of the increasing heterogeneity of student bodies in such characteristics as abilities and interests, in what ways should arrangements be altered so as to take into account this expanded range of individual differences?

(7) Are certain teaching arrangements (e.g., the fifty-minute hour) in one field (for example, mathematics) necessarily appropriate for other fields (for example, history)?

(8) Should all classes in all subject matter areas meet the same number of times per week?

(9) In what ways can the total campus environment be altered so that its peculiar forces can be useful in promoting learning?

(10) Is the current emphasis upon grades justified? How valid are many of the decisions about students when they are made on the basis of grades?

(11) Is there evidence to support the notion of the great influence which many faculty members believe they exert upon students?

(12) What is the validity of the personal-contact notion, which seems to form the basis of so many of our present arrangements—for example, advising?

(13) To what extent should students participate in important decision-making about the academic affairs of colleges and universities?

(14) "A liberal arts education seeks to create for the individual a basis for mature private life and intelligent participation in society," declares one college catalogue, typical of many others. Given the desirability of such broad goals, what do we specifically mean by them, and how effective are we in achieving them?

THE OPEN MOUTH

A few words of counsel and caution are in order for the audience we want most to reach—*new* and prospective faculty members. These words of Francis Bacon may be prophetic:

In the year of our Lord 1432, there arose a grievous quarrel among the brethren over the number of teeth in the mouth of a horse. For 13 days the disputation raged without ceasing. All the ancient books and chronicles were fetched out, and wonderous and ponderous erudition, such as was never before heard of in this region, was made manifest. At the beginning of the 14th day, a youthful friar of goodly bearing asked his learned superiors for permission to add a word, and straightway, to the wonderment of the disputants, whose deep wisdom he sore vexed, he beseeched them to unbend in a manner coarse and unheard-of, and to look in the open mouth of a horse and find the answer to their questionings. At this, their dignity being grievously hurt, they waxed exceedingly wroth; and, joining in a mighty uproar, they flew upon him and smote him hip and thigh, and cast him out forthwith. For, said they, surely Satan hath tempted this bold neophyte to declare unholy and unheard-of ways of finding truth contrary to the teachings of the fathers. After many days of grievous strife the dove of peace sat on the assembly, and they as one man, declaring the problem to be an everlasting mystery because of a grievous dearth of historical and theological evidence thereof, so ordered the same writ down.[8]

NOTES

1. A. D. Eurich, "Better Instruction with Fewer Teachers," *Current Issues in Higher Education, 1956: The Proceedings of the 11th Annual National Conference on Higher Education,* ed. G. K. Smith (Washington: Association for Higher Education, 1956), 10–16. Quoted by permission.

2. Research Division, National Education Association, *Teachers Supply and Demand in Universities, Colleges, and Junior Colleges, 1963–64 and 1964–65,* Research Report 1965-R4 (Washington: National Education Association), p. 55.

3. R. I. Evans, *et al., Resistance to Innovation in Higher Education* (San Francisco: Jossey-Bass, 1967).

4. F. Rudolph, "Changing Patterns of Authority and Influence," *Order and Freedom on the Campus,* ed. A. Knorr and W. J. Minter (Boulder, Colo.: Western Interstate Commission for Higher Education, 1965), 5.

5. J. A. Davis, *Great Aspirations* (Chicago: Aldine Publishing Co., 1964); and J. A. Davis, "Reference Group Processes and the Choice of Careers in Science" (Chicago: University of Chicago National Opinion Research Center, August, 1964, mimeographed).

6. D. L. Thistlethwaite, *Effects of College upon Student Aspirations,* USOE Cooperative Research Project No. D-098 (Nashville: Vanderbilt University, 1965).

7. Nevitt S. Sanford, ed., *The American College* (New York: John Wiley & Sons, 1965), p. v. Quoted by permission.

8. Cited in N. L. Munn, *Introduction to Psychology* (Boston: Houghton Mifflin Co., 1962), p. 4. By permission.

2

THE FLIGHT FROM TEACHING*

John W. Gardner

John W. Gardner served as President of the Carnegie Corporation and as President of the Carnegie Foundation for the Advancement of Teaching from 1955 to 1965, at which time President Lyndon B. Johnson appointed him Secretary of the Department of Health, Education, and Welfare. At present he is affiliated with the Urban Coalition of New York City. His books include *Excellence: Can We Be Equal and Excellent Too?* and *Self-Renewal: The Individual and the Innovative Society.*

The years ahead will see a rapid rise in the college-age population. The age group from 18 to 21 years provides a useful index of this rise (though obviously it does not include all college students): its number will increase from 12 million in 1965 to 17 million in 1980.

And with each succeeding year a higher proportion of the age group will attend college. In 1970, 49 per cent of the 18- to 21-year-old population will enroll in college; in 1980, it is estimated that 60 per cent of the same age group will enroll.

The resulting rise in the number of full-time college students will be dramatic. In 1965 enrollments will run something over 5,200,000; in 1980 they will exceed 10,000,000.

The figures below tell the story.

---

* This essay is not an expression of the author's personal views; it is an informal account of a discussion carried on by the trustees and officers of the Carnegie Foundation for the Advancement of Teaching at the 58th annual meeting in November, 1963.

Year	18- to 21-Year-Old Population	Per Cent in College	Estimated Enrollment
1965	12,090,000	43	5,200,000
1970	14,244,000	49	6,900,000
1975	15,768,000	54	8,600,000
1980	17,051,000	60	10,200,000

MORE STUDENTS AND FEWER TEACHERS

To predict precisely the number of college and university teachers needed in the years ahead is difficult and involves numerous assumptions, but all experts agree that there will be serious shortages in most fields. For the year 1964–65 alone, colleges and universities have been searching for 31,900 new full-time teachers; in 1969–70 they estimate that they will need 35,700.

The prime source of teachers for higher education is the graduate schools, and the doctoral output of these schools is rising, as indicated in the two fairly conservative projections below.

Year	Office of Education Estimates	National Academy of Sciences Estimates (L. R. Harmon)
1965	13,600	15,364
1970	18,300	21,548
1975	24,600	30,222

If all of those who obtained such advanced degrees went into teaching, our problem would be considerably less difficult. Unfortunately for the colleges and universities, a substantial number are drawn into nonacademic careers. Here are the percentages of new doctor's degree recipients who entered (or stayed in) teaching in recent years.

Year	Per Cent
1954–55 and 1955–56	45.2
1956–57 and 1957–58	44.5
1958–59 and 1959–60	45.6
1960–61 and 1961–62	46.7

In other words, only about half of future doctor's degree recipients will find their way into teaching, and they will be no more than a fraction of the number needed.

The shortage will be more severe in some fields and more damaging at some levels of higher education than at others. The strong colleges and universities, whose prestige and dollars will attract whatever talent is available, will suffer least. It is in the less strong institutions that the harm will be done.

MORE RESEARCH, LESS TEACHING

The failure to produce enough teachers is only part of the problem. Other factors diminish the use we are getting of those who are now in the ranks of teachers. Most important, perhaps, has been the extraordinary rise in funds available for research. Federal expenditures for research and development increased over two hundred times between 1940 and 1964:

Year	Expenditure
1940	$ 74,000,000
1950	1,083,000,000
1960	7,738,000,000
1964	14,979,000,000

For professors, research dollars mean the freedom to pursue a significant intellectual interest. They also bring the status that is associated with research grants, make it possible for the faculty member to travel, buy him free time for reflection, and enable him to attract the best graduate students and bind them to him with golden stipends. And out of his research grants come publications and promotions. It is in the nature of things that research should bring certain kinds of rewards more predictably than does teaching. The able researcher, through publication, gains a national reputation. But the able teacher is rarely known, as a teacher, beyond his own college or university. Good teaching is not only a relatively private performance; it resists measurement.

Another factor that has tended increasingly to divert time and energy from teaching is the rise in consulting opportunities with government and industry. Consulting assignments often enable the professor to perform an important service to society, and their value should not be minimized. They also enable him to add variety to his life and dollars to his income. Indeed sometimes the financial returns from such work equal or exceed the professor's salary. Most colleges and universities have been liberal in permitting outside work on the theory—often accurate—that besides serving a worthy purpose and benefiting the faculty member financially, such work enriches his teaching. But the trend toward consulting has become so marked that leading institutions are faced with the necessity of reappraising the rules under which it is permitted.

Still another factor contributing to our present difficulties is the reduction in teaching hours in many leading universities. Harold Orlans of the Brookings Institution offers the following figures:

Year	Institutions	Field	Teaching Hours
1930–31	57 Midwest colleges and universities	Sciences	19+
		Humanities	14
1960–61	12 liberal arts colleges	Sciences	12.7
		Humanities	11.2
1960–61	"eminent" universities	Sciences	6
		Humanities	8.3

Orlans reports that in three leading institutions science faculty members put in an average of only four to five classroom hours per week.

In interpreting these figures, the reader should bear three

things in mind. First, extremely small teaching loads are an attribute of the leading institutions. Second, it is by no means easy to calculate teaching loads in all cases, particularly for members of the graduate faculty who spend many unscheduled hours supervising dissertations or working in the laboratory with students. Third, the leading universities have a conception of the professor's role that requires a different calculation of his duties. These institutions believe that they are engaged in a kind of education that can only be offered by men and women who are themselves active scholars. They think of the professor as engaged one-half time in teaching and one-half time in scholarly work of his own choosing, the latter being as much a part of his duties as the former. So if a normal full-time load is considered to be twelve hours, then in these institutions the professor would be required to teach six hours.

It is not easy to say to what extent huge federal research funds have contributed to the reduction in teaching hours, but it is certain that the reduction is most marked in the "federally involved university." The competition for outstanding scholars is of course a factor. The man with a glittering reputation is often lured with the promise of minimum teaching duties. Indeed he may be given the promise that he will not have to teach at all.

REDUCING THE SHORTAGE: GRADUATE SCHOOL OUTPUT

The most obvious means of alleviating the college teacher shortage is to expand graduate school output, and few issues in higher education have received more intensive study in recent years. Expansion will occur, as indicated by the figures quoted earlier, but several factors will severely limit the rate at which it can take place. One is the teacher shortage itself: we do not have enough graduate school faculty to produce new teachers as fast as we might wish. Another is cost. The graduate student cannot be mass-produced. Each student must have a supervised research experience, which in some fields requires expensive laboratory facilities or costly field trips. In all fields it calls for a heavy investment of faculty time.

The federal government is seeking to expand the number of strong centers of graduate training, and its efforts will have substantial consequences. We need additional centers of excellence. But federal appropriations and new buildings are not enough in themselves to create an excellent graduate school. It takes the patient and devoted efforts of good faculty members—and it takes time.

A frequent suggestion for increasing the output of graduate schools is to invent a new degree short of the Ph.D. Although there seems to be little likelihood that such a degree will come into being, the argument in favor of it grows increasingly cogent. A high proportion of teachers in higher education today do not hold a doctor's degree, and it appears that in the years ahead an even smaller proportion will hold it. Furthermore, so the argument goes, large numbers of teachers are working at levels of higher education that do not really require that degree, but do require *some* well-conceived program of preparation involving both research and course work. According to the critics, the attitude of the graduate schools to these people is to pretend that they do not exist.

Most qualified observers agree that any sensible program for increasing the output of Ph.D.'s should include vigorous efforts to shorten the period between the A.B. and Ph.D. According to National Research Council data, this averages six years in the natural sciences, eight in the social sciences, and ten in the humanities. Prolonging this period is costly in every way. With each year that passes after the A.B., the graduate student is more likely to be married, burdened with dependents, and in need of substantial fellowship support. Financial pressures often force him to leave graduate work (temporarily and briefly, he tells himself) for full-time teaching, and there are no adequate inducements to encourage his return. It has been suggested that such individuals be provided with fellowships sufficiently generous to take account of their usually heavy family obligations.

ADDITIONAL SOURCES OF TALENT

Graduate Students and Emeriti. One way of adding promptly to the supply of teachers would be to make greater use of graduate students in college and university instruction. We shall deal with that possibility later.

At the other end of the age scale, more effective use of retired professors is an obvious possibility. Most institutions have mandatory provisions for retirement at a specified age—generally between 65 and 68. Some have recommended that retirement be postponed to a later year, but the truth is that while some faculty members are capable of effective work well beyond 70, others have ceased to be effective long before 65. All the facts of differential performance in later years weigh against raising the mandatory retirement age. Rather, each institution should create flexible arrangements so that the mandatory provision can be waived in selected cases. A good many institutions now have such provisions.

If the faculty refuses to accept any retirement arrangements that are not equally and uniformly applicable, then the only alternative is to let even the most vigorous go and hope that other institutions will pick them up. This is happening with increasing frequency, and the trend will almost surely continue. But there are still not adequate arrangements for placing vigorous emeriti.

Ph.D.'s Outside the University. As we said earlier, many young Ph.D's pass up teaching careers to enter industrial, governmental, and nonprofit research institutions. Any organization that harbors substantial numbers of highly qualified research personnel should find ways of making them available for teaching in collaboration with nearby universities. A number of major industrial and governmental laboratories (e.g., the Hanford Atomic Plant, Los Alamos Scientific Laboratory, and Monsanto Chemical Company) have already worked out such arrangements with their educational neighbors. Such collaboration not only makes new teaching talent available to students, but enables bright young people in the laboratories to continue their graduate work.

Women. Women who have completed part or all of their graduate work but have interrupted their careers for family reasons are another rich source of talent. It is discouraging to note that the percentage of women doctorates has fallen off considerably over the past 40 years.

A number of experimental programs are now being developed to encourage talented women to continue their education

Percentage of all Doctorates Awarded to Women	
1920–24	15.1
1925–29	15.3
1930–34	14.6
1935–39	14.8
1940–44	13.3
1945–49	13.4
1950–54	9.3
1955–59	10.5
1960–61	10.9

beyond the A.B., and there is overwhelming evidence that both the talent and motivation are there. But frequently the opportunities are lacking. Often the chief obstacle is the ridigity of graduate school rules—e.g., rules against fellowship aid for part-time students.

Other Sources. Still other sources of teaching talent for higher education are highly qualified professional people in the community and exceptionally qualified high school teachers. The latter group is already moving into junior college teaching and will do so increasingly in the years ahead.

OTHER SOLUTIONS

Enlarging the Total Supply. Industry, government, the academic world, and all the professions are competing for the same limited supply of trained talent. So sooner or later we must go behind the obvious question "How can the universities get a larger share?" to the more basic question "How can the total supply be enlarged, so that *every* field can have a larger share?"

This forces us to face the fact that we have neglected the development of existing resources of talent in our society. We lose talent in the slums of our great cities through the economic and social deprivation that blights motivation and stunts intellectual growth. We lose it when we allow race prejudice to limit opportunity for some Americans. We lose it when we accept a notion of the role of women that denies them full opportunity to develop their gifts. We lose it when bright young people go from

college directly into jobs that offer them no opportunity for
further growth.

We are just beginning to understand what we might do to
prevent such waste. It is too large a topic to be dealt with here,
but it deserves mention as a fundamental aspect of the problem.

Better Use of Present Faculty. Colleges and universities
could make better use of the talent they already have. They
could, for example, provide more supporting personnel—such
as secretaries and teaching assistants—so that precious faculty
time will not be siphoned off into clerical and subprofessional
tasks. They could provide more imaginative arrangements for
keeping veteran teachers refreshed and up-to-date. And they
could seek ways in which students could be thrown on their own
resources for more of their learning, while receiving ample
individual attention at critical points. (In a recent test of Pennsylvania State University's "pyramid plan," a cluster of undergraduates, led by a senior and supervised by graduate students
and faculty, taught themselves the course content as effectively
as it was taught in conventional classrooms and produced dis-
proportionately high numbers of majors in the subject.)

Television and programmed instruction can be used to reach
larger numbers under circumstances in which the new techniques threaten no impoverishment of the educational experience. And finally, we now know that it is possible to create
collaborative arrangements between neighboring institutions so
that they can share teaching talent and facilities in mutually
beneficial ways.

More Effective Recruitment. One reason many able Ph.D's
have been diverted from teaching careers is that the colleges and
universities have never brought to bear their full energies and
capabilities in recruiting. If they did, they might considerably
diminish the loss of potential teachers to nonacademic callings.

Off-Campus Education. Another approach to the problem is
to ask how many of the vast numbers of students headed for
college in the years ahead could be provided with adequate
educational opportunities off campus. If we could accomplish a
major improvement in our off-campus educational ventures, we

might serve large numbers of students without their ever having to crowd onto the college campus.

RESTORING THE STATUS OF TEACHING

Though all these measures may be helpful, the college teacher shortage will never be solved without an intensive and thorough-going effort to reëstablish the status of teaching. In many small liberal arts colleges no such restoration is necessary because the status of teaching has not deteriorated, but in universities the problem is acute, particularly at the undergraduate level. As a rule the university administration is so busy struggling to maintain the strength of its huge graduate and professional schools that it neglects the undergraduate. And so does the faculty. Harold Orlans writes: "A Brookings Institution survey of over 3,000 faculty members showed that in colleges as well as universities, small and large, in the humanities and social sciences as well as the natural sciences, faculty members at every rank, regardless of how little time they devoted to undergraduate teaching, wished to reduce that time still further, although all groups wished to increase the time devoted to graduate instruction and especially to research." [1]

Some graduate school professors believe that the teaching of undergraduates is such a different venture from graduate and professional education that it should be handled in a separate institution. But historically almost every effort to separate the two in this country has come to naught; most university people today believe that a single faculty should teach both undergraduates and graduates.

It would be folly to suppose that the status of college teaching can be restored without the active collaboration of the federal government. In some measure, at least, the problem stems from the enormous impact of federal grants on the academic world. Responsible university leaders agree that that impact has been on the whole highly beneficial. In the matter under discussion, however, there can be no doubt that federal grants have helped to create the problem we must now solve. And we shall not solve it until we bring about some changes in governmental attitude and practice. Putting the matter broadly, the federal government must understand how essential it is to maintain the vitality of our colleges and universities as teaching institutions. It must see that without that vitality, these institutions will ultimately be of little help to it in achieving its research and development goals.

If federal agencies ever see that point clearly, they will find ways to be helpful. Congress is reluctant to approve funds that go directly into teachers' salaries, but there are plenty of other steps that can be taken. Certainly the common practice in federal fellowships of forbidding the grantee to teach must be reëxamined; it is quite possible to devise programs of federal grants for graduate students that combine research and teaching.

But more important than any possible action by the federal government is action by the universities themselves. One aspect of the problem as it exists today is a crisis in values. The seemingly limitless supply of research funds, consulting opportunities, easy promotions, and dazzling offers has been around for some time now. There is a whole generation of able young faculty members who never knew a time when affluence did not prevail. Thus it is hardly surprising that a few of them exhibit an opportunism that startles their elders. Some of these heavily-bid-for young people appear to have no sense of institutional loyalty whatever and simply follow the offers where they lead. They regard the agencies that provide the research grants as their real sources of nourishment. Whether they correspond with the National Science Foundation from Stanford, Michigan, or M.I.T. really doesn't matter very much. In their view, students are just impediments in the headlong search for more and better grants, fatter fees, higher salaries, higher rank. Needless to say, such faculty members do not provide the healthiest models for graduate students thinking of teaching as a career.

Only a small percentage of the academic world is guilty of such opportunism, however, and the large majority who do not share this approach to life should consider the possibility of formulating ethical standards to curb the crassest opportunism in grantsmanship, job-hopping, and wheeling-dealing.

There are other things that faculty leaders, departmental

chairmen, and university administrators could do to restore the status of undergraduate teaching. They could accord both economic and status benefits to those who do unusually effective work with undergraduates. At U.C.L.A. the administration holds certain reserve funds to be distributed to those departments that demonstrate that some importance has been given to undergraduate teaching. At M.I.T. recently the Visiting Committee for Sponsored Research urged the university to be highly selective of new research projects in the future, "to ensure that the further growth of campus research makes not only its well-recognized contributions to graduate education, but also strengthens undergraduate instruction, providing the undergraduate with opportunities for participation which enrich his total educational experience." [2]

Leading universities might agree among themselves to exercise restraint in offering reduced teaching loads as an inducement to move. They might even agree that no new nonteaching faculty would be hired. (Some universities have already adopted the latter principle.) One university president has said flatly, "No one should be added to the faculty who is not willing to communicate with freshmen," but this goes further than most faculties would accept.

Another step any university can take is to make fuller use of its graduate students as teachers. Writing of Harvard's new five-year Ph.D. program in history, which includes two years of teaching experience, Franklin Ford, dean of the Faculty of Arts and Sciences, says: "We simply cannot do many of the things we want to do for students in the College unless we find ways to make more use of the *best* graduate degree candidates."

But he hastens to add that the teaching is beneficial to the graduate students as well as to the College. "We (at Harvard) are saying that, insofar as funds and classroom opportunities permit, teaching experience ought to be a part of training for the Ph.D., and that it ought to be undertaken by graduate students not as a chore imposed by financial need but as an invaluable part of their own education." [3]

One practical measure open to any university is to set higher stipends for teaching assistantships than research fellowships.

The reverse is usually true today, and the ablest students make a beeline for the fellowships.

In short, faculty and administration leaders should behave as though undergraduate teaching is important. They will be surprised how quickly young faculty members—and government officials—will get the message.

NOTES

1. H. Orlans, "Federal Expenditures and the Quality of Education," *Science,* Vol. 142, No. 3600 (December 27, 1963), 1626.

2. *Report of the President* (Cambridge: Massachusetts Institute of Technology, 1963), p. 18.

3. F. Ford, "Ph.D.'s and the College—A Quiet Revolution," *Harvard Alumni Bulletin,* October 26, 1963, 113.

3

SETTING INSTITUTIONAL PRIORITIES

Logan Wilson

Logan Wilson, President of the University of Texas from 1953–60 and Chancellor in 1960–61, is currently President of the American Council on Education. He has authored *The Academic Man*, co-authored *Sociological Analysis*, and edited *The State University*. His latest contribution is *Emerging Patterns in American Higher Education*.

The era of the Great Society is also an era of great expectations for higher education. Most of us are doubtless pleased by this enhanced status for our institutions and ourselves, and why not? For many years we professional educators have urged the public at large to raise both the level of support and the level of expectation for educational enterprise. At long last, perhaps more as a result of changed circumstances than of our own persuasiveness, the American people are sold—and maybe oversold—on the values of higher education.

Within a single generation, we have witnessed a remarkable transition. The opportunity to go to college, traditionally regarded as a prerogative of the few, is now widely viewed as a right for all high school graduates, and indeed, as a duty for the majority. Those who teach them were once looked upon mainly as schoolmasters and schoolmarms for a privileged class of adolescents, but now professorial counsel is eagerly sought by business, industry, and government.

Even though some of us may look back nostalgically to the more halcyon years, from our vantage point in the mid-sixties it is clear that higher education confronts unprecedented opportunities and is being asked to assume unparalleled obligations. Not only are colleges and universities expected to transform youths in attendance, but also to play key roles in an effort to uplift the population at large. Whether it be eliminating poverty, reducing unemployment, improving morals, or getting a man to the moon, institutions of higher education are being drawn into a multitude of public concerns.

In a complex and growing society, this is understandable. Colleges and universities cannot stand still in purpose and scope; they have an inescapable obligation to provide better education for greater numbers, to enlarge and improve knowledge, and to serve society in unanticipated ways. They must be viable institutions, and they cannot ignore current problems and issues without losing their significance in a dynamic social order.

Even so, I would caution that neither our whole system of higher education nor any of its institutions should engage in the futile endeavor of trying to be all things to all men. If we saddle our institutions with responsibilities they cannot effectively discharge or shift to them burdens which more logically belong to other agencies, we run the risk of damaging the integrity of academic endeavor and fragmenting its basic purposes. I hope we are beginning to realize that multiuniversities, like small colleges, can be overextended too, and that it is essential for us to set priorities of effort among and within institutions of higher education.

In looking at this matter of priorities, let me begin by mentioning a few things which higher education cannot do. One of them is to transform native ability. In an ever more complicated social order where there are fewer and fewer jobs for individuals with limited intelligence and little education, it is unfortunate that an impediment of birth should remain a lifetime barrier; but in a cross section of 100 persons there are about 20 whose intelligence quotients fall between 70 and 80, and several more of still lower mentality. Although the right kind and level of education can make most of them into more useful members of society, it needs to be emphasized that *higher* education is simply beyond their grasp. Between these individuals and the brighter members of our population, it is estimated that about

46 persons, with IQ's ranging from 90 to 110, come within the range of "normal intelligence." Many four-year colleges would not admit youths with this apparent potential; most of them could enroll somewhere, however, and some of them would do quite well, both before and after graduation.

To be sure, there is no better mechanism than an open educational system for distributing the members of a society according to their aims and abilities; but we must bear in mind that the bright learn more readily than the dull and hence formal education on advanced levels does not necessarily foster egalitarianism. Those who mistakenly believe in higher education as an equalizer of individual differences must therefore find other grounds for upholding the notion that everybody ought to go to college.

No matter how much we may increase our support of formal schooling on all levels, it seems to me unreasonable, moreover, to expect classroom influences to substitute for families, neighborhoods, and churches; to bear the main burden of transmuting caste into class; and to reconstruct the whole society morally and aesthetically while leading it intellectually. We must recognize that the mass media, including advertising, and the values they implicitly or explicitly endorse supply youth with many of its behavioral patterns. Other institutions must share importantly in the development of our human resources and in overcoming poverty, delinquency, and immorality.

Although it may be *infra dig* in academic circles to suggest that formal education can be overdone, I would suggest that it may be possible to have too much of a good thing even when the "good thing" is higher education. Human resources, like material resources, are subject to the law of diminishing returns; and at some point additional investment in education may make a lesser contribution to society than other forms of private or public expenditure. In many parts of the world overpopulation is a more serious immediate problem than undereducation. Even in a relatively affluent society the extension of the years of formal schooling on the one hand, and the earlier retirement and longer life of the older generation on the other, impose increasing costs on society; as more of these costs are borne by public agencies some difficult choices will have to be made among alternative uses of resources.

Turning now from these disclaimers about education as the sure road to utopia, I want to emphasize my conviction that it is undoubtedly our most effective single way to improve the general welfare. Our colleges and universities do indeed have important roles as servants and shapers of the Great Society. The utterances of educators and others are replete with statements about the services of academic institutions. Various national committees and commissions in recent years have drawn up specifications of goals for all levels of education. President Lyndon B. Johnson, more than any other President in our time, has committed his leadership to a positive educational program for the entire nation.

American higher education assuredly does not lack objectives, but one of our major current problems is what to do about pressures and priorities. What do they mean to the 2,100 or so campuses throughout the nation? *Pressures and Priorities in Higher Education* lists pressures from such sources as local, state, and federal government; the growing and changing student population; demands for continuing education; increasing costs; industry, labor, business, and professional groups; the disadvantaged; women; the various academic disciplines; international needs—and a variety of others.

Since even our so-called "private" institutions are really public service agencies, and all colleges and universities are supported by the larger society in one way or another, they can hardly ignore these pressures. Their real problem is how to serve contemporary society without becoming subservient to it. If they become mere knowledge factories geared solely to increasing human productivity and improving standards of material living, their time-honored commitment to the pursuit of truth, the advancement of higher learning, and the enrichment of our cultural heritage may fall into neglect. Are they not obligated, as Harry D. Gideonse—formerly President of Brooklyn College and currently Chancellor of the New School for Social Research —has suggested, to offset many of the influences exercised by the society itself in order to develop men and women fit for intellectual and moral responsibilities in an even better society?

When I referred to the integrity of academic endeavor I had in mind the historic fact that our leading institutions have been dedicated to high purposes, including transmission of the best that men have thought and said in the past. Colleges and universities serve by playing a contemplative and critical role, and if they become too enmeshed in daily affairs of the community at large this function is bound to be eaten away. One evidence of what is already happening is the growing phenomenon of the faculty *in absentia,* and the fragmentation of intellectual effort and professional loyalties. Student loyalties also appear to be falling away in some places where centrifugal forces are not sufficiently countervailed by institutional cohesion and consistency of purpose.

As we confront the diverse and sometimes conflicting pressures surrounding us and try to set worthy priorities for endeavor, it would be well to remind ourselves that colleges and universities are the main trustees of civilization. Adherence to this trusteeship, I would insist, has undoubtedly been a prime factor in their enduring quality as human organizations.

In addition to consistency of purpose (without which there can be no integrity), institutions of higher learning also have leadership obligations. If they are to help create a greater society and a better world, they must be able to criticize as well as comply, to shape as well as to serve. This in turn implies a reasonable freedom of choice with respect to the means and ends of higher education.

With these provisos ever in view, let us now focus attention on the broad problems of setting institutional priorities. Here I think we should reverse our usual approach and start with higher education as a whole rather than with individual institutions. Our past assumption has been that the separated aims and activities of existing colleges and universities would somehow add up to the best educational interests of the nation. In my judgment, this is no longer a valid assumption. Higher education has become too complicated, too costly, and too important in the national welfare for its basic decisions to be made haphazardly.

For a number of years my conviction has grown that one of higher education's most urgent needs is for coherent, unified planning. My conclusion is that we have entered an era when colleges and universities must cease to be a mere congeries and that they must somehow become a genuine system characterized by unity no less than diversity. In my opinion, there is no other way to expand and improve our institutions without an enormous waste of time, money, and effort. I set forth some of the particulars of this matter several years ago in a paper on "Basic Premises for a National Policy in Higher Education," [1] and I have noted with interest that Mr. Conant's recent book, *Shaping Educational Policy*,[2] deals with similar considerations.

Although I endorse Mr. Conant's proposal to use state governments as units to form an "Interstate Commission for Planning a Nationwide Educational Policy" for our public schools, the private sector's importance in higher education suggests to me that on upper levels it would be more feasible to work through a nonpolitical arrangement. An advantage of this approach is that it would build upon existing structures and utilize more fully the leadership of professional educators in setting and implementing priorities.

Whether enough educators are willing to subordinate their vested interests in particular departments, disciplines, projects, and institutions to place the common or national interest paramount remains to be seen. T. R. McConnell's view is that interinstitutional coordination is effective only when compulsory. And I agree that politically prompted schemes of mandatory coordination are pushing educators into thinking more realistically about the give-and-take of interinstitutional cooperation.

As was shown at the annual meeting in 1964 of the American Council on Education, traditional forms of institutional autonomy are being displaced by emerging patterns which emphasize interdependence rather than independence in the expansion and improvement of colleges and universities. Consortia, statewide and regional systems are evidences of a new era in the governance of higher education and reflect an inescapable need to think beyond the confines of a single campus in allocating priorities of educational effort.

The growth of federal aid to higher education in the fifty states has also led to the necessity for the establishment of central agencies, such as commissions, to determine institutional and program priorities. Although the academic community at large still uses divergent approaches to Congress, the American Council on Education is endeavoring to develop a more unified front, and each year it formulates and distributes widely a statement of program priorities. Neither the Council nor any other single agency can claim to be the one voice speaking for all of higher education, of course, but I am hopeful that we can reduce the babel of voices being heard in Washington and reach more agreement about how the pressures on higher education can be channeled constructively.

One of our current difficulties, it seems to me, is a reluctance in educational circles to face up to the need for a more logical division of labor among institutions to counteract indiscriminate local responses to pressures for proliferation. Despite our lip service to diversity and pluralism, it looks at times as if we were trying to homogenize higher education. One manifestation of this is the "university syndrome" which in effect means that a single institutional model is imitated so indiscriminately that many campuses begin to lose their unique character and purpose.

I would not argue that uniformization in higher education is invariably bad, but I do contend that variety of form and function is useful and should be maintained. Junior or community colleges, for example, can hardly serve their distinctive purposes if appreciable numbers of them yield to pressures to become higher level institutions. Liberal arts colleges, technical institutes, and other distinctive kinds of higher learning centers also have important functions which may be submerged if too many of them are transmogrified into so-called universities in response to local and popular pressures.

The pressure for funds also is tending to homogenize the support and control of our institutions as more and more public institutions seek to augment their budgets from private sources and more and more independent institutions rely increasingly on tax support. There are advantages to any institution in varied support, of course; but if forms of support and control become too mixed everywhere, then the duality of American higher education may be lost.

In short, a unified system of higher education should also be diversified, with each type of institution playing a distinctive role in the whole division of labor, and each having a unique character. All colleges and universities may share in varying degrees the collective functions of teaching, research, and public service; but every place needs its own priorities. Our common ends may be almost infinite, yet the local means to pursue them are always finite.

Even a Harvard or a California has to make decisions about the kind of clientele it wishes to serve, the caliber of faculty it wants to maintain, and the range of programs it will or will not carry forward. Where resources are more limited, operations should be within more restricted ambits, with no institution undertaking more than it can do well.

Since institutional mistakes in determining their priorities stem more commonly from overweening than from modest ambitions, it seems to me that many campuses would benefit from more insistence on adequacy and less rhetoric about excellence, more underpinning for basic programs and less dissipation of resources in a multitude of projects, more attention to strengthening the citadel of higher learning and fewer sorties in the countryside.

All of this may seem unduly conservative, but in my judgment the first order of business for administrators, faculty, and students alike is to foster the best possible campus environment for learning. Commenting on some current aspects of student behavior, Sidney Hook noted in *The New York Times Magazine* (page 18) on January 3, 1965:

> They cannot be encouraged too much to broaden their intellectual interests, and they certainly must not be discouraged from giving expression to their generous enthu-

siasms for civil rights, for human welfare, for peace with freedom. But good works off campus cannot be a substitute for good work on campus. Ultimately, the good causes our society always needs have a better chance of triumphing if their servitors equip themselves with the best education our colleges and universities can give them.

Our primary obligation to students in residence implies a top priority for the teaching function. As I have said elsewhere, there is a danger in many places that the student, and particularly the undergraduate, may become the "forgotten man" as our institutions become increasingly involved in such off-campus concerns as aiding various levels of government with political problems, meeting miscellaneous demands for continuing education, lending staff personnel to the developing nations, and so on. These and many other endeavors have strong claims for academic attention, but in my opinion never to the extent that basic on-campus obligations come to be neglected. I would also add that because of our reluctance in academic circles ever to drop anything or anybody—from an unneeded course to an unwanted professor—some of our priority problems are self-made.

Research should have the next priority in many, but by no means all, institutions. In the foreseeable future I doubt that our nation needs or can fully support more than 40 or 50 really distinguished, research-oriented universities. Such centers should be more numerous and more widely dispersed than at present, but it is not only wasteful but also futile to think that every locality should aspire to having one or more. Although research of the kind that contributes to the advancement of knowledge should be a major emphasis in perhaps 200 of our institutions, I believe that on most campuses it is sufficient to expect the average faculty member to keep abreast of his field.

Since real creativity in research is a very scarce talent anyhow, I think that most faculty persons would benefit themselves and their institutions more by devoting greater effort to the improvement of teaching. Contrary to the "publish or perish" myth that is much talked about of late, in all except a few leading institutions less than ten per cent of the faculty accounts for ninety per cent or more of all published research. My recommendation would be that we reduce the strain on the majority, trim the output of needless publication, and upgrade the quality of instruction by a more realistic adjustment of the talents available.

Insofar as research involves the production of new knowledge of theoretical or practical significance rather than keeping oneself well informed about a field, however, it does entail an institutional commitment of time and money as well as talent. It therefore follows that many kinds of research cannot be conducted by the faculty in their spare time with the same libraries and laboratories they use for undergraduate teaching.

For the institution with a heavy commitment to research, there are many kinds of policy questions to be answered. Who should make the decisions about the kinds of inquiry to be undertaken? What criteria should be used in selecting or rejecting proposals? Is the distinction between basic and applied research meaningless, and if not, does an academic institution abuse its societal role by engaging in development projects? Does the individual researcher owe his first loyalty to his college or university, to his discipline, or to the funding agency? To what extent should the availability of funds determine the directions of research? In answering these questions, it seems obvious that the institution with no priorities of its own will be the place where outside pipers will call the tune.

Although I would assign a third-rank priority to what is usually called "public service," I would remind you that teaching and research are themselves public services of indispensable importance to the larger society. Those miscellaneous other outside involvements that we have come to designate as public service are now considered to be legitimate claimants for faculty and staff attention. Beginning with the president, public service demands upon him are often so numerous and so pressing that he functions only residually as an educational leader on his own campus. Other staff persons and many faculty members are also likely to be drawn into a gamut of peripheral service activities having to do with everything from the local Chamber of Commerce to the most distant foreign country. Indeed, if all the outside demands were met—and few of them can be readily brushed aside as unworthy—nobody would be left on many campuses except students and custodial workers.

To my way of thinking, every institution needs therefore to engage continuously in a reassessment of its end and means. It must ask itself such questions as these: Is this service important or merely urgent? Would it strengthen or weaken activities with higher priorities? Can another agency do it just as well, or better? To be sure, a new project may be of special interest to the bursar's office or the public relations bureau, but we keep telling ourselves and others that capable academic personnel are in short supply. If this be true, then there ought to be devils' advocates in all institutions to deal with the proliferation of services.

In concluding these remarks, I realize that at times I may have seemed to reflect the conscience of an educational conservative. If so, this has not been my intention, for I am a staunch believer in an enlarged and enhanced role for higher education as a prime mover toward the Great Society. As someone has aptly said, colleges and universities are the engines of modern civilization. I am confident that we can continue to step up their power and increase their load capacity. If we are to make them the main vehicles of social progress, however, I would urge their users to know where they want to go and to choose the main roads rather than the byways to get there.

NOTES

1. L. Wilson, Unpublished lecture delivered to a Seminar in Higher Education at Harvard University, July, 1962.

2. J. B. Conant, *Shaping Educational Policy* (New York: McGraw-Hill, 1964).

4

YES, JOHN,
THERE ARE TEACHERS
ON THE FACULTY

William R. Hutchison

William R. Hutchison, Professor of History and American Studies at
American University, has taught at Yale University and Hunter College,
held a visiting appointment at the University of Wisconsin, and for
the 1966–67 academic year was at the Charles Warren Center, Harvard
University. He is author of *The Transcendentalist Ministers* and a
contributor to *The Utilization of Teaching Resources*.

Editor John Fischer of *Harper's* not long ago asked the
plaintive question whether American university faculties include
persons interested in teaching (*Harper's Magazine,* Vol. 230,
No. 1377 (February, 1965), 18). As he said, the impression
is abroad that they do not. "That muffled snarl you hear is the
sound of unhappy college students enrolling . . . for the Spring
semester." All across academia, as we have now repeatedly been
warned in 16-point capitals, self-interested professors are glut-
ting the highways in their Flight from Teaching, while back on
the campus the discontent of "cheated students" turns to revolt.
Whether one is more distraught about The Plight of the Small
College or about The Shame of the Graduate Schools is likely to
depend upon which of the large-circulation magazines has arrived in the morning's mail.

Some of the recent jeremiads go so far as to foreclose the
possibility of either repentance or salvation. According to this
cataclysmic view, the destructive effects of mass education have
been such that all efforts to improve the quality of college
teaching are "foredoomed to failure." We can never, it is said,

reinstate in democratic modern America the favorable educational conditions of those halcyon days when only four per cent of our youth attended college. "What is distressing," in the loftily weary words of Professor Andrew Hacker of Cornell, "is that so many students, faculty members, and observers of the educational scene still think that serious reforms are possible."

If attempts at reform are going to distress Professor Hacker, he is in for a good deal of suffering. Although Americans have a reputation for discussing their relatively placid national experience in the terminology of crisis, plight, and watershed, it is difficult even to get a respectful hearing for the language of cataclysm and utter despair. Most of the educational critics, together with their readers, will continue to propose and expect serious improvements.

Their confidence will be allowable in view both of America's past history and of her present resources. Although our difficulties today may differ in form from those surmounted in earlier periods of American higher education, they are scarcely so alarming as the problems faced—to take one of the milder examples—in the first twenty years at Cornell University. And more recent history gives considerable cause for encouragement. The numerous experimental programs initiated by the Fund for the Advancement of Education and by other foundations in the 1950's have demonstrated the value of honors programs in enriching the curriculum for the ablest students; they have shown in fact that "independent study" and cross-disciplinary courses can be highly valuable to the nonhonors student. Other reformers, such as the leaders of the Danforth Foundation, have sought to combat the harsher effects of that "impersonality" that can be either the greatest strength or the chief weakness of the large-university setting. And student reformers, aided by sensitive leadership from national student organizations, are now bidding fair to provoke in two years more improvements in the training and evaluation of classroom teachers than their elders have implemented in two generations.

Up to now, however, most of the hopeful experimenting admittedly has provided little relief where the shoe is pinching most grievously—in the largest of our universities. Michigan and some others have established "honors colleges"; and the success of these, together with the longer-standing success of similar programs elsewhere, makes it frivolous to talk as though the percentage of American youth engaged in serious intellectual training has been declining. We should be wary, as James A. Perkins has warned, even of desiring to return to some "academic Walden" which may never have existed. Unquestionably, though, the ordinary, able, unspectacular student in the large university is at this moment getting less than he has a right to expect; and if he shows a youthful rebelliousness, or never develops an enthusiasm for the enterprise of learning, we should not be too surprised. We have not yet discovered how to transfer some of the known techniques of effective teaching from the relatively benign situation of a few small or very wealthy institutions to the less yielding atmosphere of those large and hard-pressed universities in which the great majority of our students are now enrolled.

Even here, Mr. Fischer's kind of plea, for all its stridency, that something must be done, will continue to be more persuasive than Professor Hacker's advice that nothing can be. But what, precisely, can be done? The answer currently most popular, because it seems so uncomplicated and offers such identifiable villains and heroes, is that we can curtail "research." We can insist that professors stay on campus and teach their students. We can increase the rewards for good teaching, and can encourage the students to help us expose bad teaching.

The net effect of two years' public clamor along these lines may turn out to be positive; yet the usual anti-research argument is enfeebled for any useful function by its grave misunderstandings of the educational scene. In fact, if there is an award this year for the slogan that has most confused the public dialogue, "publish or perish" should be in the running. This phrase, originated years ago by wronged academics to explain the personnel policies of American universities, has now been taken up by press and public as the quick answer to what is wrong with teaching. Even the judicious Mr. Fischer can repeat the canard that "no faculty member (with rare exceptions) is rewarded if he teaches well, or punished if he doesn't."

Inferior teaching is not going to be corrected by diagnoses that are even more inferior; and the anti-research diagnosis applies remotely, if at all, in the case of ninety-five per cent of our institutions. Some 2,000 of the 2,100 colleges and universities could scarcely be staffed at all if appointment, retention, and promotion depended upon quantity of scholarly production. These institutions make little attempt to insist upon publication, although promotion may well be more rapid for the ablest scholars and slower for those who publish nothing. As the dean of an excellent municipal college put it: "When a department's recommendation of a member for tenure is supported by publication, it goes through; when it isn't, we talk about it." The talk may end in firing; but far more frequently, provided the candidate is a good teacher, it ends only in a year's or two years' delay in his promotion to permanent status.

Nor does the "publish or perish" explanation of things serve very well for those large and leading institutions to which the critics are chiefly referring. The criteria actively in use in these institutions do include good teaching and do involve qualitative standards for judging achievement in research and writing. The list of "mere teachers" passed over for places in the most prestigious universities is indeed long and honorable; but so is the list of producing scholars sent packing by leading academic departments. That there are many posts for which "only producing scholars need apply" is perfectly true. A graduate institution that aspires to train research workers and writers as well as teachers must be staffed, if possible, by persons with experience in all of those areas. But this does not mean that the merely quantitative "producers" are the ones most likely to succeed in their applications. Deans and department chairmen in these institutions can confirm, by showing who has been hired and who fired over a period of years, that the rewards for mere busyness in producing undistinguished research are about on a par with the rewards for a shallow popularity in the lecture hall. In both cases, superficial work undoubtedly is rewarded more often than it should be, but is rewarded far less often than the current stereotype would suggest.

One of the problems about our public dialogue in this area is that the public has been trained to think of research as an occupation that may be glowingly successful or may be a shameloos boondoggle, but in either case is quite inessential to the main business. "The business of teachers," as the saying goes, "is to teach!" ("Dammit!" normally is added.)

The academics so far have offered little response. The usual answer from that quarter makes research sound like an intellectual sauna bath, a way of keeping the tired academic mind in trim. Rarely do the defenders mention more concrete connections between research and teaching, perhaps because these are too obvious. The fact is that no very vital instruction of any kind can be carried on without scholarly books and the studies and monographs that undergird them. And this is as true in the more recondite fields as it is in Current Events or Engineering: One is not likely to be able to teach about ancient China with only the books of the 1920's, any more than one could teach geology or physics with only the books and charts of the 1920's.

If the scholarly work must be done and synthesized, it is reasonable to ask who should sponsor this work if not, primarily, the universities. Many complaints about the usurpations of research in the university program seem to harbor an assumption that all that sort of thing should be sponsored by the Rockefeller Foundation and the Sloan-Kettering Institute, so that the universities could be left free for something quite separate called teaching. Under such a dispensation, the students who are now allegedly "in revolt" because they see so little of the well-known Dr. X—and see so much of his graduate assistants—would presumably be contented. They would have neither Dr. X nor his graduate students, all of whom would be over at Sloan-Kettering doing cancer research.

We should be cautious, however, about accepting the premise—so surely and impressionistically asserted—that students are getting inferior teaching from the more "productive" of their mentors. There is, first of all, the rankling fear that even the best students may misjudge the teachers who will mean most to them. (George Bancroft in 1820 gave a low rating to Professor Hegel at Berlin, and to the entire faculty at a depersonalized university called Göttingen.) But we should also ask whether the students actually are turning up the good scholar/bad teacher syndrome with a regularity that would suggest any correlation at all.

The responses to my own very preliminary inquiries at institutions where student evaluations have been running for as many as thirty years suggest that we should look carefully at any alleged negative correlation. If research activities have really been doing more harm than good to classroom teaching, the student surveys and student recommendations for good teaching awards do not seem to show it. Most of the respondents to my inquiry in fact shared the view of Dean Pearson of Bennington, who commented as follows on Bennington's thirty-year experience with student ratings: "The overwhelming evidence is that those faculty members who rate highest with the students are the most productive scholars in their field. There are exceptions of course, but there is no doubt whatever of the predominant tendency."

None of my respondents leaned toward an opposite view. And none of the several studies, from 1929 to the present, which have touched upon this matter, has supported an opposite view. More work is needed on the relations between effectiveness in research and effectiveness in teaching; but unless the evidence changes drastically colleges like Bennington will continue to feel justified, when they must choose between two teachers of equal merit, in betting on the long-range teaching effectiveness of the more productive scholar. And surely it will not be ridiculous for the leading universities to demand that their permanent positions be held by good teachers who are also conducting research of high quality. Bear in mind that the aspirant for tenure, unless he can be induced to commit murder or seduce his undergraduates—and even that may not be enough to oust him—is going to be around for life. His appointment in all probability precludes any other in the same field for thirty years.

In the sponsoring of research, just as in an investment in the work of businessmen or lawyers, risks are high and wastage inevitable. In spite of all efforts to discourage frivolous or opportunistic work, we shall probably continue to have bad briefs, wasted business trips, and useless scholarly articles. But returns may easily be proportional to risk. While a classroom teacher, with luck, will exert a useful influence upon several dozens of students in a year's time, one first-rate book will affect thousands directly, and will have incalculable effects through the other works that it stimulates. The pressure on academics to bring out unripe works of scholarship can be real enough, and damaging; but the corrective does not lie in devoting fewer resources to research. What is needed is a deployment of funds—and incentives—that will encourage the long-range effort and discourage the potboiler.

The anti-research arguments, therefore, deserve a less central place than the one they have enjoyed in the current debates over the quality of college teaching. The positive ideas that usually have accompanied them are certainly in order—the various proposals made by Mr. Fischer and others for the better training, auditing, and rewarding of classroom teachers, and for condemning the disdain-for-teaching pose as the peculiarly bad joke that it is. Yet without more fundamental reforms in the structure of our academic life, large doses of such good intentions will go down like the pep pills the students take to keep themselves awake, and will have exhilarating effects of about the same duration. The current "revolt" will achieve little unless it can manage to unseat two tyrannous habits which have been criticized repeatedly but are still saucily in power. The first of these is the lecture-course approach to learning, the second what may be called, with some understatement, the seven-ring semester.

Despite patient advocacy and convincing results, in recent years, from the champions of "independent study," the prevailing motto in our universities continues to be *Nihil Sine Orationibus:* "If you haven't had a lecture course in it, you haven't learned it." Most departments therefore attempt to offer lecture courses in all fields in which their undergraduate and graduate students are expected to develop a competence. This in turn means, in all but the most fully staffed universities, that the departments must sponsor lectures not just on those subjects in which their members are specialists, but on all subjects of which any member has any knowledge. What is more, the lecturer on any subject is generally expected to "cover" it, not just to speak on the portion he knows best.

Breadth in a teacher is of course much to be admired, and a well-trained scholar can usefully teach elementary courses, guide reading, or even supervise graduate research in fields outside his specialty. The scholar in ancient or medieval history may conceivably "keep up," in a rough sort of way, in such fields as modern European history. But by and large the teacher who attempts to give forty lectures a semester on a subject not his own is wasting a vast deal of everyone's time. No matter how able, he does not have the expertise to write lectures that in any significant way go beyond what the students can read in the most readily available textbook. If he is good enough he can vivify this or any subject by his personality, but even so his talents are not being used to best advantage. All the vividness, moreover, may depart from him if he is asked, as are younger scholars everywhere, to change fields every time an area is—God forbid—not "covered."

Even the omnicompetent and the inexhaustible are usually giving too many lectures per week to do their students much good. It is not uncommon for clergymen to feel that one twenty-minute sermon deserves two days' preparation. Academic lecturers, working with less divine and no secretarial assistance, probably should not inflict fifty minutes of scholarly material upon their students without equivalent preparation. Teachers, like ministers, may be forced to use old lectures without revising them (revising can easily take one day per lecture), but surely this is not something our system should encourage. The common practice, therefore, of requiring college teachers to give from six to fifteen public lectures per week is a way of insisting upon mediocre performance.

Whatever other teaching and advising he does, both in his specialty and outside it, the college professor should be running no more than one lecture course at a time; and the student should be making proportionately greater use of the supervised and tested reading list as an educational device. Then, instead of forcing the lecturer, as we now do, to summarize what is avail-

able in the libraries and bookstores, we might insist that he give
lectures that his colleagues as well as his students would attend
because these lectures would represent the outthrust of his
scholarship—his exploration of new ideas or bringing together
of older ones. Lecturing of this kind admittedly could become
too specialized for the undergraduate student, but this need not
be the case. The teacher, given time to prepare, can also find
time to know what his students have read and can keep in
communication with them.

The viciousness of the bad-teaching cycle becomes more obvious when one observes the current textbook market. The kind
of "coverage" provided in lecture courses is available not just in
one text but sometimes—as in American history—in more than
thirty substantially identical texts, almost any of which will do
for introductory purposes. Nowhere, probably, do we have more
wastage per cubic foot of scholar than in the devotion of vast
quantities of "research" time to the rewriting of textual materials and the rearranging of documents. Each publisher, of
course, yearns to have his very own—and, as the blurbs say,
"unique"—edition of virtually the same book. Computers could
do this endless reshuffling very well, and sometimes would do it
more honestly; but the scholar has to waste his time on it
because, frankly, baby needs shoes.

If it is the huge introductory courses in the universities that
create this affluent but bizarre situation, one might become
curious as to why the students in these courses could not be sent
to real books—especially in view of their not being given real
lectures. One trouble is that real books demand a reader's time;
and in the universities as elsewhere we live in the age of the
memo. Students, to a sorry extent, are precluded from real
reading because, along with everything else, they must run
around to fifteen lectures a week to hear their textbooks summarized.

This brings up the second obstacle to a general improvement
of teaching: the seven-ring semester. The principle of the
seven-ring semester is that "all types of academic activity must
be carried on simultaneously." When institutions change from
the semester system to quarters or trimesters, as many have

done, or from a five- to a three-course arrangement, they nearly always take along this sacred doctrine and enshrine it in the new calendar. The fundamental dogma is that the student must be kept off balance by having his time atomized as much as possible. His resources must be divided not only among a number of courses and their requirements, but between long-range and short-range obligations, and between the curricular and the extracurricular. If the academic terms are shortened, then the student must be made to attend more lectures per week in each course. Under no conditions must he be allowed to cease his frenzied activity and concentrate on any one thing until a few days before the final examination—if then.

At first blush, "independent study" seems the answer to this foolishness, both for the professor and for the student. But independent study programs, designed in part to free the time of teachers, have often confounded their sponsors by eating up more faculty energies than do the regular procedures. The smaller or richer institutions can sponsor these programs any- way, and have done so, much to the profit of their students. But few institutions of any size have managed to allow more than a pitiful two weeks' "reading period" at the end of a frenetic semester.

The student's long-range work of reading important books, writing papers, and preparing for examinations should have more than two weeks of his uncluttered time. Whether he takes three courses or five, it would be far better for him if, after an eight-week term of lectures and discussions and quizzes, his classroom commitments were sharply reduced; he should spend the next seven or eight weeks fulfilling requirements of reading, research, and examination for which counseling help would be steadily available.

We are scared to death to do anything like this; and our reasons are those both of the Calvinist and the cost accountant. American students, we say, are too naughty and immature to be trusted with this kind of freedom. They just wouldn't do the work. More alarmingly, they would go home, or to Bermuda, and would not pay the freight in the dormitories. In such objections we have a further large field for discussion about the quality of the American undergraduate—both as he is and as he might be if we expected more of him. But for present purposes let us assume the worst about the American student. Where such must be assumed, the requirements in the form of reading lists and papers and examinations must be correspondingly rigorous. And since, on the cost-accounting side of our lives, we do need to keep the dormitories full, students under such a system might have to contract for their dormitory space for a year or a half year at a time, just as they do now.

Americans are also concerned, of course, about full utilization of classrooms. The college building in America is considered the counterpart of the factory, where utilization must be maximized, rather than of the church, in which we tolerate some under-use for the sake of higher utilities. But our universities, under the kind of plan suggested here, could provide for "independent study" and still, if they felt they must, maintain full classroom utilization. At any given time in the academic year, roughly half of the university community—both student and faculty—would be engaged in the lecture-course and seminar kind of work, while the other half would be engaged in the duties associated with "independent study." Classrooms and laboratories could, if necessary, be constantly in use by one group or the other.

Doubters will be certain that this plan, with its "supervision of independent study," would require prodigious amounts of faculty time and therefore be unworkable. My figuring does not support this. At a large state university, I taught, with the help of graduate assistants, two lecture courses for a total of 350 students. Had we, after seven weeks, discontinued lectures and discussions, and sent the students off with reading lists, my assistants and I, without increasing our working time, would have had some five hundred man-hours at our disposal over the following eight weeks. This would have been enough not only for the reading of papers and examinations, but for three individual counseling sessions for each student during the eight-week period. If a student's independent work in two areas can be consolidated, or if the advisees can be seen in groups, the time available for supervision under such a plan can be considerably increased.

The traditional lecture-course method and the fragmented academic program, both widely accepted as necessary evils, are really unnecessary evils; but they cannot be stamped out separately. Or so the experience of the last two decades has seemed to demonstrate. Without the release of the professor from most of his formal lecturing, "independent study" can never be properly supervised for more than a small elite of students. Without a willingness—at least sometimes—to let the student concentrate his efforts, a quarter or trimester system solves no problem more basic than an undergraduate's yearning for a carefree Christmas.

But, put together, calendar reform and the deflating of the lecture system might place even the most crowded universities in a position to demand good teaching and high student performance. Details must vary widely, but the key figure is a teacher who gives two—or at most three—eight-week courses of lectures per year. During each of the eight-week terms in which he is lecturing, he is also conducting seminars or discussion groups.

During the terms in which he is not a lecturer, his entire teaching time is given over to those activities that the professor now must crowd into office hours and spare moments: the prescription of reading lists, the setting and reading of major examinations, and the counseling of students on their research topics. If his students, or some of them, require constant incentive and supervision, then their tests and reports are spaced out through the term instead of being concentrated at the end. But neither the professor nor his assistants are running seminars and tutorials; they have had eight weeks in which to lay the bibliographical and other foundations for what the student is now doing.

During this same "reading term," the professor's nonteaching time goes to his own research and to his coming lectures. They are closely allied. If he is any good, he is being given a chance to show it, and his students will have no impression that his research somehow cheats them of the benefits of his teaching.

This ideal-sounding teacher and scholar is, fortunately, not missing from the academic scene even today. The scandalously generalized nature of recent criticism makes it especially important to affirm that models for schemes like the foregoing are scattered all through American higher education. But we could ensure that more teachers, on more faculties, would represent the type. This in turn would help assure that higher education, which survived when Americans were poorer and more ignorant, can adjust to conditions of high literacy and affluence.

5

THE USES AND ABUSES
OF NEGATIVE RESULTS

Howard E. Gruber

Howard E. Gruber directed a recent large-scale investigation of instruction in higher education at the University of Colorado. He was Professor and Chairman of the Department of Psychology at the New
School for Social Research from 1963 to 1966, at which time he became Professor of Psychology in the Institute for Cognitive Studies at
Rutgers University. His research interests include perception, thinking,
and the history of science. He is an editor of *Contemporary Approaches to Cognition* and *Contemporary Approaches to Creative
Thinking.*

In the history of science, negative experimental results
have sometimes had a profound influence on subsequent
thought. Galileo found that the weight of a body had no effect
on its earthward velocity; Weissman found that chopping off the
tails of rats had no effect on tail-length in subsequent generations. Although these investigators reported "no significant
differences," their findings changed the course of science because the then prevalent theories predicted a difference. Unhappily, this particular bond between experiment and theory is not
to be found in contemporary investigations of self-directed
study.

This report discusses research on self-directed study, with
special emphasis on two major findings. First, when the criterion
for evaluating self-directed study is the student's learning of
subject matter, the results are indeterminate, producing no very
powerful argument for or against self-directed study and no
argument for or against conventional methods such as lecture
courses meeting two or three times per week. Second, when the

criterion for evaluation of self-directed study is a group of attitudinal changes such as increased curiosity, critical thinking, and attitude toward independent intellectual work, brief experiences with self-directed study do typically produce small, favorable changes. From these results it may be argued that a systematic educational program can be worked out, viewing the four-year college experience as a unified opportunity for growth toward intellectual self-reliance. In this paper, a sequence of attitudinal and cognitive changes is proposed, and some attention is given to the changed role of the college teacher in such a program.

Broadly speaking, research on self-directed study is concerned with all methods of higher education designed to increase the student's responsibility for his own education. But among such methods, this report is not primarily concerned with *independent study,* a term usually reserved for those teaching methods involving individual projects in which student and teacher are in a one-to-one relationship. As described by Bonthius and others,[1] independent study is very rewarding, but it makes prohibitive demands on faculty time. We are concerned, rather, with those ways of increasing the student's responsibility for his own education which preserve the essence of the course system, the one-to-many relation between teacher and students. For want of a better term, we refer to such methods as *self-directed study.* Although these methods vary, investigations of self-directed study have one essential point in common: while preserving the course system, the proportion of time devoted to formal classroom meetings is reduced.

Research workers in the field and in the laboratory recognize that educational experiments in self-directed study fail to yield dramatic or even consistent results. In the face of negative results (i.e., "no harm done"), many educators cling to their belief in the efficacy of lectures or other formal classroom meetings; likewise, many psychologists optimistically cling to the hope that a convincing demonstration of the efficacy of self-directed study is "just around the corner."

During a protracted investigation of student-centered teaching methods which included self-directed study, McKeachie was forced to conclude that such methods are "no panacea" for the problems of higher education.[2] Further, his important review of research on instructional methods stresses the predominant theme of "no significant differences" among educational methods.[3]

Similarly, after a three-year investigation of self-directed study in many different university courses, Gruber and Weitman were forced to the rather weak conclusion that as far as learning of conventional course content is concerned, "a reduction in attendance at formal classes to one-third the usual number resulted in either small losses or small gains, the gains being somewhat more common than the losses."[4]

However, the failures to find striking superiority of self-directed study should not be interpreted as representing empirical support for the unfounded American decision to subject college students to some 2,000 lectures in four years. If anything, field studies conducted at Antioch College, the Universities of Colorado and Michigan, and elsewhere around the country do justify reduction in the number of formal class meetings. Such reduction produces little or no loss in subject matter learned, and almost certainly does produce some improvement in attitude toward independent intellectual work, as well as in curiosity and critical thinking.

The major findings emerging from such field studies may be summarized as follows: a small change in the fabric of a student's life produces only a small change in his intellectual development. However, it should be stressed that all of these field studies have been extremely restricted, even timid, in character. On the surface, reducing the number of lectures attended in a course from three per week to one per week may seem a drastic change. (We even eliminated all lectures in one experimental group with rather favorable results.) Actually, when the experiment is restricted to a single course in a single semester, the change can be described as a temporary reduction from 15 to 13 lectures per week—not at all a fundamental change in the student's intellectual way of life.

These field studies are limited in two other ways. First, the student's work is typically still fragmented into five or six

courses per semester. Second, having had years of training in
certain teacher-directed patterns of education, the student is
perfectly capable of privately preserving these patterns, at least
in large part, unless far more drastic changes in his situation are
introduced, or, alternatively, unless training methods are developed deliberately to break up these patterns. Given a textbook,
a course outline, and an impending final examination, there is
nothing to prevent the student from re-creating and maintaining
the passive, cramped, teacher-directed study pattern to which he
has long been accustomed. Indeed, since he has four or five
nonexperimental courses to cope with at the same time, the
student in the experimental group often sees his only salvation
in resisting whatever temptation to strike out on his own the
self-directed study course may offer him. Much of our interview
material suggests that this is actually the case,[5] and Campbell's
more restricted laboratory experiments suggest a similar conclusion.[6] For if the American college student has learned little else,
he has learned the strategy of passive acquiescence in uncritically assimilating the material the teacher thinks is important.
This is a strategy that *works*: it has gotten him where he is, and
it has gotten his older brother a little further on the road to the
sort of success they are both striving for.

Taking note of the slightly positive but relatively unimpres-
sive results of field investigations of self-directed study, Campbell attempted to maximize the effect in a more carefully controlled study, resembling a laboratory experiment. Emphasis
was placed on equating the materials used by different groups,
using each student in both self-directed and teacher-directed
methods, and conducting both methods of instruction under
individualized learning conditions to avoid the confounding of
certain variables. In spite of all these precautions, Campbell
arrived at a conclusion strikingly similar to the closing paragraphs of most field studies:

> Finally, it is worth noting that in no experiment did
> self-direction have an adverse effect on learning. This is
> economically quite important, for if there is nothing to be
> lost in learning efficiency, self-direction could save a good

deal of time and money. . . . Learning efficiency too might show greater gains over a period of years than we have demonstrated in our brief experiments, at least for students who are motivated to learn. . . the cumulative effect on his problem-solving, decision-making, and creativeness might be impressive.[7]

Although the author has no quarrel with these remarks, which he might almost have written himself, he finds it thought-provoking to notice that yet another investigation of self-directed study has ended in slightly favorable results which are suggestive but not convincing. Before educational policy-makers are willing to support radical innovations, they rightly require evidence that the proposed changes are genuinely worth the trouble that all changes cause—not merely assurances that the changes do no harm or unsubstantiated hopes that if continued long enough they *might* do considerable good.

Most research on educational method has been restricted to the piecemeal comparison of methods in a single, one-semester course, or in a fragment of such a course. Where the criterion variable has been assimilation of subject matter, a wide variety of methods has proved roughly interchangeable—methods as disparate as many lectures, a few lectures, instructor-led discussion, instructor-less discussion, individual study with little or no guidance as to sequence or timing of material, and tightly programmed instruction. Slightly "positive" results (i.e., favoring one method) in one study are balanced by slightly "positive" results (favoring another method) in another study. In short, success in meeting the criterion of coverage of course content provides no firm basis for choice among teaching methods.

Perhaps the reason for this negative result is really very simple, and all we need to do is to abandon our cherished belief that different educational methods have different effects. But it is also reasonable to consider the possibility that these experiments have left the essential features of higher education intact, for in almost all these studies the following variables have not been touched: (1) the student's academic work is divided into five or six courses per semester; (2) the teacher plans the course without consulting the student; (3) the student is given no new orientation in the educational aim of becoming educationally independent; (4) the student is given no specific instruction in active modes of thought which might transform his behavior while he is studying; (5) the immediate aim on which all students are necessarily focused is successful performance on a final examination and a satisfactory grade in the course; and (6) the person evaluating the student's performance is the teacher. Operating within situations that are alike in these essentials, the student studies in approximately the same way, whether the material is presented in the form of a lecture, conventional textbook, list of readings, or programmed textbook—he decides what the teachers want him to know and he tries to learn it with a minimum of distraction. Conclusion: "promising results in the expected direction, but no significant difference."

When we turn to effects of self-directed study other than the learning of course material, the so-called "collateral learning" of critical and independent intellectual attitudes, the results are somewhat more hopeful. Again, the changes may be small, not actually transforming the student's way of thought, but they do seem to be consistently in a favorable direction. Perhaps the most uniform finding of research in this area is that students initially *dislike* greater responsibility but come to accept it in the course of a semester, and that their brief experience with self-directed study does produce a more favorable attitude toward independent intellectual work. This result is stressed by Gruber and Weitman,[8] and similar findings are summarized by McKeachie.[9] Of course, there is little reason to believe that a single brief experience with self-directed study in an educational atmosphere fundamentally hostile to intellectual independence [10] will produce attitudinal changes of great longevity. A fuller discussion of the relation of various educational methods to the student's "image of man" and to his image of himself has been presented elsewhere.[11]

These two major findings can be summarized as follows: Exposure to a single self-directed study course produces little or no effect on the learning of course content, but it does fairly consistently produce a small improvement in attitudes toward independent intellectual work.

Let us now consider a hypothesis stemming from the *joint* implication of these findings. Attitudinal changes develop rather slowly; moreover, they are a necessary *prerequisite* to stable changes in intellectual work habits. Otherwise the student will relapse into the pattern of passive acquiescence whenever pressures mount, or whenever such patterns produce workable solutions. Furthermore, the student may need specific training to develop new patterns of active intellectual work.

What would a thoroughgoing program look like, self-contained within the college years, but stressing the protracted nature of development toward self-reliance?

The first phase in such a program would be to develop techniques for reorienting the student as soon as he arrives at college, so that he abandons any expectation that he can succeed in academic work merely by frenzied efforts to assimilate everything he is expected to know. We may not know how to do this in a way that would really reach the incoming student, but the results mentioned above suggest that we might learn to produce favorable changes in these attitudes in one or two semesters.

The second phase, overlapping the first, and lasting about a year, would be a deliberate attempt to inculcate new patterns of intellectual work. One useful guide can be found in Torrance's and Harmon's work, in which they experimentally induced assimilative, critical, and creative learning sets in different groups of students.[12] Campbell's recent study also provides some interesting suggestions on specific means of giving students brief practice in effective methods of self-directed study. The design of Campbell's study provides clearcut evidence for the hypothesis that changes in attitudes and work habits must precede self-directed study if the latter is to produce improved learning of substantive material. Campbell's findings led him to conclude that "the first obstacle to be removed in making self-direction successful is the students' strong habit of passive acquiescence."[13]

Recently, my students and I have encountered a striking instance of highly educated individuals' spontaneous tendency to utilize passive learning methods in circumstances where very simple instructions can eliminate this tendency and thereby produce dramatic improvement of performance in a simple memory task. We have been elaborating the work of Wallace, Turner, and Perkins on paired-associate learning with brief instruction in the use of an active, highly flexible mnemonic procedure.[14] In one such study, mature college graduates, all with responsible positions in educational systems, were exposed to paired-associates for eight seconds per pair. In the control group, given no special instructions, no subject spontaneously employed a successful mnemonic procedure: all behaved in a relatively passive, rote fashion. In the experimental group, given only a few minutes of special instruction, performance was better than twice as good. The point at issue is not only the value of active cognitive processes but the success of years of education in *suppressing* active intellectual work on the part of the learner.

Self-directed study must mean more than a simple alteration in the formal structure of higher education, such as can be accomplished by reducing the number of formal contact hours or the number of courses. If the student is not led to internalize new patterns of active thought, changes in the macrostructure of education may leave the all-important microstructure intact. Research on students' thought processes in the classroom, however, suggest that the obvious formal changes do facilitate new and more active ways of thinking.[15] The next step remains to be taken: to develop methods of evoking more active thinking *outside* the classroom.

The third phase of such a program would be to change the actual conduct of higher education in order to provide the student with convincing evidence that intellectual habits of passive acquiescence are bound to fail. The systematic introduction of instructional techniques placing greater and greater responsibility on the student, in such a way that intellectual self-reliance becomes a *powerful tradition*, is the most powerful force at our disposal.

But to accomplish this aim it is necessary to persuade the faculty that their students can benefit from such approaches. A prevailing faculty mythology insists, in effect, that students at the bottom of any given segment of the educational ladder are less self-reliant than students at the top. Thus, high school seniors are often given notably more mature and independent forms of intellectual work than college freshmen, and the same pattern repeats itself in the transition from the senior year in college to the first year in graduate school.

Another similar feature of the prevailing mythology is the widespread faculty belief that only intellectually superior students can profit from self-directed study. Recent research lends little support to this hypothesis.[16]

In one sense, persuading the college faculty of the value of self-directed study should not be too difficult. Frequently, a single experience in an experimental course has a marked positive effect on the professor's views.[17] With a group of high school teachers as subjects, Gruber has also demonstrated that a brief training seminar can produce measurable shifts away from dogmatic teaching and toward problem-oriented teaching.[18]

But in another sense, changing the prevailing style of instruction can be expected to be extremely difficult for a number of reasons. First, the will to effect such changes deliberately is tempered by a due regard for democratic process and a justified hesitance to interfere with the work of other individuals. Second, the legitimate desire to prepare college students for graduate school inhibits change. The educational researcher may assure his colleagues that moves toward self-directed study will do no harm, but the responsible professor wants stronger assurance than that before he initiates fundamental changes. Third, the prevailing course system makes it difficult for the professor to give the student an opportunity for self-directed study while at the same time preserving the professor's opportunity to speak his own piece, to make his own ideas felt in the student's development. A change from the pattern of five three-credit courses per semester to three five-credit courses (or even four four-credit courses) would provide a much greater measure of flexibility in combining the professor's desire to "profess" with the student's need to develop independently.

Regardless of the specific methods adopted, it is clear that no important change in the conduct of higher education can be accomplished without wide and deep faculty support. The faculty must be convinced of the feasibility and desirability of a coherent program for developing their students' intellectual self-reliance. They must also be given an opportunity to discuss and indeed to refashion their own role in the educative process. If, for example, the student were attending three formal class meetings per week, each lasting two hours, instead of fifteen one-hour classes, the teacher's role would be profoundly changed. The nature of this change has yet to be spelled out.

A program such as the one outlined above has two further difficulties that merit discussion. First, there is little firm evidence that it would actually produce clear-cut effects. If experiences at institutions such as Goddard College were more widely known, many educators would probably be convinced as to the feasibility (i.e., "no harm done") of many innovations. But this kind of feasibility argument falls far short of the positive demonstration necessary to convince educational policy-makers to inaugurate controversial changes. Such positive demonstrations can only be provided by a new kind of multi-institutional research program combining the precision of experimental control with the scope of field investigations. Although a full discussion of this approach is not presented here, I believe that such an approach is feasible and desirable, and that it would produce new insights into the process of higher education.

A second difficulty in any full-scale program for developing intellectual self-reliance stems from the long-range developmental character of this aspect of personal growth. Failure to examine these developmental implications might lead us to a peculiar impasse in which we manage to invent a program for maximizing intellectual independence and then discover that, after all, such a program results in a highly objectionable state of affairs.

It is plain to see that maximal independence is only an *intermediate* goal. If the student were to remain in such a solipsistic state indefinitely, we might begin to complain that he was an asocial recluse. We do not want to substitute the hermit's cave for the anthill. Our aim is not independence for its own sake. For this reason, in improving our methods of developing intellectual self-reliance, we must give deeper thought to the kind of human relationships our educational methods foster. Increasing self-reliance need not produce increasing alienation. Instead, it could produce a cyclical shift in the student's social role. For example, the more advanced student could exercise and deepen his own knowledge by imparting it to others. This oscillation between the role of student and the role of teacher may, in the long run, become the essential characteristic of self-directed study.

NOTES

1. R. H. Bonthius, F. J. Davis, and J. G. Drushal, *The Independent Study Program in the United States* (New York: Columbia University Press, 1957).

2. W. J. McKeachie, "The Improvement of Instruction," *Review of Educational Research,* No. 30 (1960), 351–60.

3. W. J. McKeachie, "Procedures and Techniques of Teaching: A Survey of Experimental Studies," *The American College,* ed. N. S. Sanford (New York: John Wiley & Sons, 1962).

4. H. E. Gruber and M. Weitman, "The Growth of Self-Reliance," *School and Society,* No. 91 (1963), 222–23.

5. H. E. Gruber and M. Weitman, *Self-Directed Study: Experiments in Higher Education* (Boulder, Colo.: University of Colorado Behavior Research Laboratory Report No. 19, 1962).

6. V. N. Campbell, *Self-Direction and Programed Instruction for Five Different Types of Learning Objectives,* Technical Report AIR-D10-12/63 TR (b) (Palo Alto, Calif.: American Institute for Research, December, 1963).

7. *Ibid.,* p. 16.

8. Gruber and Weitman, *Self-Directed Study.*

9. McKeachie, *The American College.*

10. Cf. Gruber and Weitman, *Self-Directed Study.*

11. H. E. Gruber, "Education and the Image of Man," *Journal of Research in Science Teaching,* No. 1 (1963), 162–69.

12. E. P. Torrance and J. A. Harmon, "Effects of Memory, Evaluative, and Creative Reading Sets on Test Performance," *Journal of Educational Psychology,* No. 52 (1961), 207–14.

13. Campbell, *Self-Direction.*

14. H. Wallace, S. Turner, and C. Perkins, "Preliminary Studies of Human Information Storage," University of Pennsylvania, December, 1957 (oited in Millci, Galanter, and Pribram, *Plans and the Structure of Behavior* [New York: Holt-Dryden, 1960]).

15. B. S. Bloom, "Thought Processes in Lectures and Discussions," *Journal of General Education*, No. 7 (1953), 160–69; and Gruber and Weitman, *Self-Directed Study.*

16. Gruber and Weitman, *Self-Directed Study;* and McKeachie, *The American College.*

17. Gruber and Weitman, *Self-Directed Study.*

18. H. E. Gruber, *Science as Thought: A Study of Nine Academic Year Institutes for the Training of Science Teachers* (Boulder, Colo.: University of Colorado Behavior Research Laboratory Report No. 16, 1961).

6

TWO BASIC NEGLECTED PSYCHOEDUCATIONAL PROBLEMS

Sidney L. Pressey

Sidney L. Pressey, currently Visiting Professor at the University of Arizona, was Professor of Psychology at Ohio State University from 1921 until his retirement in 1959. His research activities in the field of educational psychology have extended over his professional career. He produced one of the first "teaching machines" during the 1920's.

At the present time, some 50,000,000 persons in this country go to school, with approximately 5,000,000 in higher education. This is over a fourth of the population. Professional or technical training may now extend education through almost half the average lifespan; the median age of obtaining the doctorate in psychology has recently been 31, and it is higher in many other fields. All over this country billions of dollars are being spent for more buildings, equipment, and teachers to keep more people in school longer. Surely it is appropriate now to bring together any evidence as to how long people *should* continue in school, and (if this seems desirable) how progress through school might be facilitated or schooling made more efficient. Might there not be something of a breakthrough in psychoeducational methodology, markedly increasing educational efficiency, and shortening overlong programs?

HOW EARLY, RAPIDLY, LONG?

Research going back over thirty years has shown that bright children entering school at five or finishing elementary school in less than the usual time did well in high school, were more likely to go on to college, did well there, and were well-adjusted. Terman found that his gifted youngsters who finished school at 16 or younger did better in college and were more likely to graduate than those finishing older, though there was little difference between these groups in childhood IQ.[1] Research going back fifty years has repeatedly concluded that students entering college young (as at sixteen instead of the modal eighteen) are more likely to graduate, less often become disciplinary problems, and as often participate in student activities as those entering older; that students graduating young (as at twenty instead of the modal twenty-two) have the best academic records and are more likely to go on for advanced study. Several investigations have agreed that able students who have finished a four-year undergraduate program in three calendar years (a few in two) have done better academically than cases paired with them as to initial ability—even though the available methods for accelerating most wisely were not used.

All this is generally known. Perhaps not sufficiently considered, however, is the latter type of finding: In experiments where accelerates have been paired with nonaccelerates of equal initial ability, the accelerates have done better. Various studies have suggested that more education brings about more mature functioning of general ability; conceivably more education in a given time might accelerate that increase. Anyhow, acceleration seems tonic, and continuingly so. Thus, the youngsters under subvention of the Fund for the Advancement of Education (FAE) who skipped the senior year of high school (and some the junior year also) to enter college at a median age of sixteen instead of the usual eighteen, not only did much better there than the average college freshman but better even than freshmen paired with them as to ability; as sophomores, the accelerates averaged better on the Graduate Record Examination than first-year graduate students and again surpassed their controls of presumed equal ability.[2]

Moreover, sundry studies going back some forty years agree that accelerates are especially likely to be successful in careers. Two 1925 papers reported that those in *Who's Who* with an undergraduate degree obtained it about a year and a half younger than then usual, and those in that roster with the doctorate similarly had earned it early. Those men in Terman's gifted group who graduated from high school youngest most often later became vocationally outstanding. Alumni records of a New England college and a Midwestern state teachers college showed that those graduating at twenty or younger were more successful in careers than graduates at the modal age of twenty-two. A sampling from a recent American Psychological Association *Directory* gave thirty-one as median age of obtaining the doctorate; however, the last twenty-five presidents of the Association earned the degree at a median age of 25.7—E. L. Thorndike at only twenty-three and Köhler at twenty-two. Analogous data for chemists, sociologists, economists, and political scientists showed the presidents of their national organizations similarly getting the Ph.D about five years younger than the generality of their members. A sampling of members of the American Academy of Science had received the degree at a median age of 26.1, and Nobel Prize winners in physics and chemistry at a median of 25.0.[3]

Why this apparent advantage in early beginning of career? A great variety of evidence indicates that the young adult is most healthy, physically strong, able to sustain work, alert, of strong interests, intellectually creative. Lehman's recent paper on this topic shows that outstanding contributions in physics and chemistry were made most often at ages twenty-five to twenty-nine.[4] To use these years of greatest potential simply in prolonged going to school may be not only wasteful of that potential, but even harmful. In answer to an inquiry about his having obtained the doctorate at the age of twenty-three, a former president of APA and specialist in child development, now an administrator in a famous university, wrote: "I think it almost criminal to let people stay in the social role of student any longer than absolutely necessary. The longer they remain students, the longer they remain subordinate, passive, always looking up to others instead of out toward the horizon for themselves." And a psychiatrist in another university declared that "the longer the educational process, the more it tends to select men who secretly

want to escape external reality"; [5] the "protracted quasi-adoles-
cence" delays emotional maturation.[6]

It is commonly accepted that, at about the age of six, the
average child is, in abilities, personality, and need for enlargement of experience, ready for school, and that schooling should
not long thereafter be delayed. Should a later developmental
stage be recognized when the young adult is ready for and in
need of self-realization, as in marriage and career—a status also
best not long delayed? Relevant here may well be the recent
great increase in number of married students, though cramped
finances and career uncertainties might seem to make marriage
and families seem unwise. Might it conceivably be desirable that
the law require not only the beginning of full-time schooling at
six, but its ending, say, not later than 26?

Nevertheless, an outstanding public school system, with many
advanced secondary school courses into which able students
may "accelerate," yet declares against early high school graduation. A famous Eastern university, which has been giving advanced placement credit, is introducing special courses for such
students so that they will not finish in less than four years, even
though about eighty per cent of its graduates go on to graduate
or professional school. In the educational Wonderland, one
must now run faster to remain in the same place! In 1957 a
committee of graduate school deans stated that obtaining the
Ph.D. now commonly takes six or seven years, but should not
take more than three.[7] On the other hand, a conference on
graduate training two years later did not make length of such
training an issue.[8] In a striking editorial in *Science*, Dael Wolfle
declared that "It almost seems as if a conspiracy existed to delay
the age at which the formal educational system lets go of a
young scientist and allows him to be on his own." And Wolfle
specifies the delay from the first grade (half as many children
now enter that grade at five than twenty years ago) to the
doctorate (now taken a year later than formerly) and, increasingly, a postdoctorate to delay further.[9] Surely here is a basic
psychoeducational problem of pervasive importance; the program of these meetings shows it now largely neglected.

TEACHING, AUTOMATION IN TEACHING, AND LEARNING WITHOUT TEACHING

If progress of able students through school should be facilitated, how may this be done? Certain means have already been mentioned or are well known: entrance at age five or into the second grade, progress through the six years of elementary or secondary school in five, shortening of undergraduate programs through credit by examination, "all-year" schooling (really only about ten and a half months), and heavier academic loads. Certain other possibilities may be added here.

In the recent *Handbook of Research on Teaching*, the chapter on college teaching mentions two experiments in which students who never went to class did best on the final examination.[10] A recent report is confirmatory. One large section of a first course in psychology never met after the first two weeks of planning sessions, but simply took weekly tests on each week's assignments. If anything, these students did a little better on the final examination than another section having the usual two-hour lecture and one quiz session each week. Further, more of the nontaught section bought supplementary reading matter and later elected another course in psychology.[11] Probably not only the instructor but also his students saved more time than was evidenced, since most of them could probably study-read a given amount of matter faster than he could lecture it. Granted that the final examinations may have been too narrowly informational, do not such experiments raise basic questions as to the adequacy of largely taken-for-granted procedures in teaching, at least at the college level?

If the instructor in the above experiment had used a self-scoring auto-instructional weekly test in his nontaught section, he would have saved much more time, and the nontaught students probably would have done better. Or such brief teach-tests, used frequently in the regular section, would probably have aided it in doing better yet. The important advantage of the small class is the possibility of much student response with confirming or corrective feedback—which objective teach-tests can provide.

For example, a simple, inexpensive three-by-five card now available makes multiple-choice tests self-scoring and instructional. The card has thirty rows each of three small black dots, in two columns. Each student is given such a card and a sheet of not more than 30 three-choice questions keyed to the card's right-answer pattern. The directions tell him to erase the second dot in the first row on the card if he judges the second alternative to the first question right. If it is, he will find an "R" under the overprint; if he does not, he should reconsider and try again until he does find the right ("R") answer. He thus erases his way through the test, the feedback differentiating for him the wrong from the right answer to each question. When he finishes, he counts his wrong erasures to get his own error score. The card is a very convenient compact detailed record, and the test sheet can be used again.

Materials of this general type have been used in regular class hours as check tests and study aids, and found significantly to raise grades on midterm and final examinations. Such materials have also guided superior students so effectively, in study for credit by examination and in independent-study laboratories, that everyone finished the twelve-week course in six weeks or less and with high grades (many then taking another course in similar fashion the second half of the quarter). Many also mentioned both gains in ability to work independently *and* more acquaintance with other students and the instructor because of the small-group informality.[12] It would seem evident that such a teach-test was a convenience for a teacher (since the tests are scored in the taking), and for each student a great help since, as he answers each question, each right answer is at once confirmed as such, and each mistake at once so designated with immediate positive guidance. Yet such teach-tests, to aid use of established instructional matter, have been almost entirely neglected in the past few years because of the great interest in programming. The author urges that some of you try such teach-tests or "adjunct autoelucidation."

The previously cited psychology class which never met was really an instance of guided independent study that was planned in the initial two weeks and checked in weekly tests. Successful experiments with independent study date back over twenty-five years and have repeatedly demonstrated that, with appropriate planning, many students are able to learn as well with much less class time than has customarily been required of them. As mentioned above, autoinstructional tests may here help greatly. Leaders in secondary schools are urging that time in independent study may there total up to 40 per cent for some pupils.[13]

A month in Washington for a student of government, or a semester in Mexico as aid in learning Spanish, would probably be acknowledged as valuable. For a student preparing to teach, work in summer camp may be very worthwhile and deserve credit. Perhaps many would agree that more use should be made of work and travel in education.[14] A secondary school may have trips and arrange for educationally significant summer work in local industries. Perhaps a revision of the *Handbook of Research on Teaching* will add a chapter on how to learn with less teaching, or none!

WHAT POSSIBLE FACILITATIONS? GAINS?

Judgment is ventured that: With wise use of present-day methods of appraisal, guidance, instruction, and such flexibilities as the nongraded form of organization, a fifth of the children in most elementary schools could finish a year earlier than is now usual (and more finish high school); that a similar proportion of secondary school graduates could complete that six years in five (and more go on to further education); that at least a third of all college students planning graduate or professional training should finish that four years in three or less—and that the graduate deans were right in asserting that about three years is usually enough for the doctorate. Further judgment is made that, if such means for facilitating progress through school had been available, most readers could, desirably, have completed their education and begun their careers at least three years earlier than they did.

A medical discovery which adds years to life is universally acclaimed. Educational procedures which might add three years to professional careers in the young prime of life are surely important. More generally, if from elementary through graduate school many youngsters might save one year of schooling (and some, two or three), many millions in school costs might be saved, and possibly more in "earnings foregone." [15] Throughout, the educational climate might be much improved if all understood that, as a student did well, he could save time.

For many, therefore, the question implied in the first paragraph of this paper must be answered in the affirmative: Initial full-time education *is* greatly overextended for some. But for many others, education does not go far enough; facilitating their educational progress would lead many of these to go further. Even those who have reached that peak and presumed terminal of higher education—the doctorate—should not stop there. As Robert Oppenheimer has remarked recently, "Nearly everything that is now known was not in any book when most of us went to school; we cannot know it unless we have picked it up since." [16] Initial professional training cannot be adequate for long; better a three-year doctorate followed by professional refresher programs, as in medicine, law, and industrial technology. Most colleges and most public school systems seem little aware of the great need for adult education, nor do investigators now show much interest in a field where Thorndike pioneered over thirty-five years ago—adult learning. Only under pressure of a national emergency have educational efforts focused on schooling of the grossly underprivileged. Though sometimes overextended, American education is not overexpanded; it has far more than enough unfinished business.

Facilitations of the progress of able students like those described are possible by means now commonly available in terms of usual periods of instruction and academic calendars. But by far the most effective practical experiment referred to above freed itself of all that: Students in the independent study laboratory came in when they wished for as long as they desired, to work with others or alone, taking teach-tests as appraisal and guidance was needed, consulting with the instructor as need was felt. As noted earlier, all these students finished the course in half the usual time or less, doing well. Surely in our own undertakings we desire to work intensively and get things done; how exasperating if we had to drag out every task through a semester—and listen fifteen hours a week to people like us!

Probably such intensive work, thus aided, greatly favors effective learning of structured meaningful matter; probably there should be bold action research trying out such procedures in elementary courses. But, again, such research seems comparatively neglected. If more use were made of relevant travel and work, and of the "all-year" school (made more tolerable if so diversified), then much time might be saved—with more adequate learning. Many more students might, like Thorndike, obtain the undergraduate degree at twenty and doctorate at twenty-three; and perhaps more, beginning their careers thus early, might approach him in productivity!

RÉSUMÉ

This essay seeks to highlight the importance of two psychoeducational problems now comparatively neglected. The first grows increasingly urgent as more young people flood into our colleges and more of these go on to some form of advanced training; half a lifetime may go by before one can begin his lifework. Such prolonging of education is becoming taken for granted—encouraged with increasingly generous stipends and literally built into our campuses, as in housing for married students.

The second problem concerns use of such aids as autoinstruction, such procedures as guided independent study, and such administrative structures as the nongraded school and all-year calendar. These aids and plans might primarily be used to enrich or to accelerate. If used wisely in this last way, they might largely solve the first named problem, save billions of dollars, remake American education, and have worldwide significance.

NOTES

1. L. M. Terman, *The Gifted Group at Mid-Life*, Vol. V, *Genetic Studies of Genius* (Stanford, California: Stanford University Press, 1959).

2. Fund for the Advancement of Education, *They Went to College Early* (New York: FAE, 1957).

3. S. L. Pressey, *Educational Acceleration: Appraisals and Basic Problems* (Columbus: Ohio State University Press, 1949); and

Sidney L. Pressey, "Educational Acceleration: Occasional Procedure or Major Issue?" in *Personnel and Guidance Journal,* Vol. 41 (1962), 12–17.

4. H. C. Lehman, "The Relationship Between Chronological Age and High Level Research Output in Physics and Chemistry," *Journal of Gerontology,* Vol. 19 (1964), 157–64.

5. L. S. Kubie, "Some Unresolved Problems of the Scientific Career," *American Scientist,* Vol. 40 (1954), 106.

6. *Ibid.,* p. 112.

7. M. E. Hobbs, "Doctors and Masters—Good and Bad," *Proceedings of the Ninth Annual Conference of the Association of Graduate Schools* (Columbia, Mo.: Association of Graduate Schools, 1957), pp. 35–38.

8. A. Roe *et al.,* eds., *Graduate Education in Psychology* (Washington: American Psychological Association, 1959).

9. D. Wolfle, "Delayed Independence," *Science,* Vol. 143 (1964), 104.

10. N. L. Gage, ed., *Handbook of Research on Teaching* (Chicago: Rand McNally, 1963).

11. O. Milton, "Two-Year Follow-Up: Objective Data After Learning Without Class Attendance," *Psychological Reports,* Vol. 11 (1962), 833–36.

12. A. A. Lumsdaine and R. Glaser, *Teaching Machines and Programmed Learning* (Washington, D. C.: National Education Association, 1960); and Sidney L. Pressey, "A Puncture of the Huge 'Programming' Boom?" in *Teachers College Record,* Vol. 65 (1964), 413–18.

13. B. F. Brown, *The Non Graded High School* (New York: Prentice-Hall, 1963).

14. S. L. Pressey, "Psycho-technology in Higher Education versus Psychologizing," *Journal of Psychology,* Vol. 55 (1963), 101–108; and J. W. Wilson and E. H. Lyons, *Work-Study Programs* (New York: Harpers, 1961).

15. T. W. Schultz, "Education and Economic Growth," *Sixtieth Yearbook of the National Society for the Study of Education* (Chicago: University of Chicago Press, 1961), pp. 46–88.

16. R. Oppenheimer, "The Tree of Knowledge," *Harper's,* Vol. 217 (October, 1958), 56.

7

TEACHERS AND TEACHING

Ruth E. Eckert and Daniel C. Neale

Ruth E. Eckert is Professor of Higher Education at the University of Minnesota. She has been a member of the Educational Policies Commission, the Executive Committee of the Association for Higher Education, and several other national committees. Her publications include *When Youth Leave School, Outcomes of General Education, Higher Education in Minnesota* (ed.), *A University Looks at Its Program,* and *Job Motivations and Satisfactions of College Teachers.*

Daniel C. Neale is Associate Professor of Educational Psychology at the University of Minnesota and a member of the staff of the Center for Research in Human Learning. In his work, he emphasizes the relationship of experimental psychology to problems of teaching.

Although swiftly mounting college enrollments have alerted even the lay citizen to the great shortage of faculty members and the consequent need for instructional adjustments, research on these problems continues to be restricted in scope and, in many instances, in imagination and scientific rigor. Of the several hundred articles and brochures published since 1960 on staffing and teaching problems, most describe current or recommended practices or urge a greater concern for quality—but they provide few principles to guide this quest.

Contributions of the period include significant ideas regarding theory and experimental design, an encouraging upsurge in a few types of studies, and occasional investigations which have set new and fruitful patterns for research. One hopes all these will stimulate better studies in the future. Some references are included here because of research merit; others suggest trends or illustrate the nature of the uncited literature.

THE COLLEGE TEACHER

Spurred by a prospective need for 35,000 new faculty members annually in the late 1960's, a number of studies have probed the career decisions, preparation, status, services, and satisfactions of college teachers. A Western Interstate Commission for Higher Education symposium on *Studies of College Faculty* [1] and articles by Adelson,[2] Katz,[3] and Knapp[4] competently interpreted earlier findings and charted the way into this rich but largely unexplored territory.

Recruitment. A well planned study by Gustad, based on questionnaire and interview data from college teachers and former teachers in selected fields in the Southeast, indicated that many people get into college teaching by "drifting" rather than by deliberate design.[5] Eckert and Stecklein, who studied Minnesota faculty members,[6] and Hartung, who investigated graduate students and college teachers of biology in the Northeast,[7] reached a similar conclusion. Of special interest to future researchers is Medalia's critical review of three variables—"career decision," "occupational image," and "institutional potency"—involved in recent studies of faculty recruitment.[8]

Interest in college teaching as a possible career appears to have increased substantially among undergraduate students during the past few years. O'Dowd and Beardslee found that students in five Northeastern colleges had a well defined and attractive image of the college professor and compared him favorably with all other major professional groups,[9] a finding also stressed by Corcoran[10] and Kinnane,[11] both of whom reported serious consideration of this field as a career.

Preparation. Although the controversy continues regarding appropriate graduate training for college teachers and some new programs have been instituted, evaluative studies are still lacking. Berelson concluded, from the extensive factual data and opinions gathered in his study of graduate education, that the current research-oriented Ph.D. program can properly continue to serve both the prospective teacher and investigator.[12] In contrast, McGrath supported his plea for special programs for college teachers with information gathered from several hundred college presidents concerning shortages or lacks in graduate training.[13] Recent efforts to study this situation by field, illustrated by Hartung, who investigated biologists,[14] and Perkins and Snell, who examined the opinions and professional achievements of historians,[15] should throw more light on this problem. A survey by Ewing and Stickler revealed that 91 leading universities—more than triple the number involved two decades ago—were currently offering courses on college teaching or other phases of higher education.[16]

Orientation and In-Service Training. In a carefully designed study using questionnaires, supplemented with interviews in selected institutions, Tracy found that practically all accredited North Central colleges provided some faculty orientation. Half of these programs had been initiated recently, however, and very few were well developed.[17] McCall [18] and Gustad,[19] who also investigated orientation practices, confirmed Tracy's conclusion that new teachers in particular need help on instructional problems. Exploring role conflicts and congruences through successive interviews with new faculty members in a single institution, Allen and Sutherland similarly underscored institutional responsibilities for staff orientation.[20] Only Miller and Wilson surveyed longer-range faculty development procedures, in a study of small Southern colleges.[21]

Status and Services. Reports issued biennially by the National Education Association, Research Division [22] and the U. S. Office of Education [23] on the size, composition, and academic and economic status of the profession have improved steadily in quality and furnish valuable descriptive information for researchers. Also useful is the recently completed survey by Ingraham and King of "outer fringe benefits" in colleges and universities.[24] Whether judged by salaries paid, associated benefits, degrees held, academic rank, or social esteem, the academic man is relatively better off than he was a few years ago. Bernard's study, which arrays evidences from statistical, biographical, and personal-documentary studies, competently correlates and interprets current knowledge about women faculty members.[25]

Few investigations of the character and scope of faculty services have been reported recently, beyond those made for purely local use. While the largest share of time is typically invested in teaching and related student services, the pattern varies significantly by institution and academic rank. Some recent studies suggest a marked movement of major staff members in large universities away from undergraduate teaching,[26] but in most types of colleges it is research and scholarly writing rather than teaching that tend to be crowded out by other responsibilities. Stecklein[27] and Doi[28] have perceptively reviewed earlier efforts to measure faculty load and have suggested some refinements in techniques.

How faculty services should be evaluated continues to be a lively but not a seriously researched problem. The difficulties are well outlined in a study by Gustad, who asked administrators throughout the country about the criteria they used in deciding upon academic promotions. Although teaching effectiveness received top mention, the six kinds of evidence used most often in judging this were all of the "hearsay" variety.[29]

Satisfactions. As Medalia noted, studies of faculty satisfaction and morale need to be more clearly conceptualized.[30] Differences in methods used may also partially account for the picture emerging from the study by Gustad which is less optimistic than several other recent studies. While most faculty members seem to like their jobs, a few leave the profession, probably because of motivational factors as well as unsatisfactory pay or work conditions,[31] and others shift positions, as Stecklein and Lathrop showed in their pioneering attraction-retention study at the University of Minnesota.[32] Sagen, using Murray's "needs-press" framework in investigating faculty satisfactions, found that both personality traits and institutional variables are significantly related to satisfaction with present position,[33] a conclusion also supported by Allen and Sutherland.[34]

In general, recent studies of prospective and current faculty members have yielded illuminating knowledge regarding their backgrounds and current status, though much less has been learned about their interests, outlooks, and satisfactions. Judging from the literature, little study has yet been given to their roles, as individuals or organized groups, in the academic community. But promising hypotheses developed in these exploratory expeditions should, if pursued, yield knowledge about faculty comparable to that now available for college students.

COLLEGE TEACHING *

Unquestionably the finest single source for researchers interested in instructional problems is the *Handbook of Research on Teaching*, which provides excellent discussions of theories of teaching, designs for research, and measures of teaching and learning. Three decades of college instructional studies are incisively analyzed and interpreted in the concluding chapter, by McKeachie.[35] In another useful volume, *Theories of Learning and Instruction*, current knowledge about learning is reviewed and its relationship to teaching discussed.[36] Popularly written interpretations of recent studies, including some that do not reach regular publication channels, are provided in the U. S. Office of Education's "New Dimensions in Higher Education" series, edited by Hatch.[37] A second supplement prepared by Eells extended through 1961 his invaluable annotated bibliography, *College Teachers and College Teaching*, raising the total references covered since 1945 to 5,656.[38]

Concepts and Theories of Teaching. A persistent criticism of research on teaching methods is that too often it has not been related to an adequate theoretical framework. Presumably, the latter would help to clarify teaching method variables, relate learning theories to the complexities of educational settings, and stimulate more comprehensive studies of college teaching. In line with current efforts to develop such a framework for the entire field of education, Smith has re-examined the concept of teaching and suggested a fruitful model for studying "episodes" in the teaching cycle.[39]

* This review was undertaken while the junior author was supported in part by grants to the University of Minnesota, Center for Research in Human Learning, from the National Science Foundation, the National Institute of Child Health and Human Development, and the Graduate School of the University of Minnesota.

The actual development of teaching theories remains in its infancy—not a surprising finding, since such development must draw extensively from research and theories in the youthful behavioral sciences. In this connection, Gage recommended that more use be made of prominent learning theories, e.g., identification, conditioning, and cognitive theories.[40] Little application of the concept of identification has yet been reported, but conditioning theory has provided an important guide to research on programmed instruction. Drawing upon Gestalt theories of learning, Ausubel has set up a series of controversial hypotheses about the teaching of verbal knowledge and supported some of these in pilot experiments with college classes. An interesting aspect of his theory is its stress upon the limitations of "discovery" approaches at the college level.[41]

Several paradigms for research suggested in the *Handbook of Research on Teaching* hold considerable promise for developing and testing such theoretical formulations. McKeachie [42] and Siegel and Siegel [43] have also argued persuasively for frameworks which relate measures of the college environment, personal traits of teachers and students, and method variables to instructional outcomes and which encourage study of their complex interactions. Preliminary experimental tests support such a wide-angled approach.[44]

Although current teaching theories do not as yet have many implications for instructional practice, they are already serving as a promising guide to research. As these theories are expanded and refined through more vigorous experimentation, the relation of the behavior of teachers to the learning and personal development of students should become better understood.

Teaching Methods. No recent studies have surveyed the methods that faculty members generally are using in various types, sizes, and levels of classes to find out what innovations or adaptations have occurred with skyrocketing enrollments. And little new has been reported about the effectiveness of lecture and discussion methods; this lack probably reflects disenchantment with earlier studies. Experimental manipulations and comparisons of student-centered and instructor-centered classes also have waned. Independent study, which McKeachie characterized as one of the "glamour methods of the 1960's," also received less attention than might have been expected. In contrast, the literature on programmed learning increased strikingly, and many studies, though of a somewhat different character than earlier ones, were made of televised instruction. An important influence on the course of research appears to have been the funds available for specific types of studies.

Lecture and Discussion Methods. No research projects comparable to the 1957–59 Miami University study of large-group teaching procedures [45] have been reported recently, but scattered comparisons generally support its findings that neither the initial acquisition nor the retention of learning is substantially affected by teaching method. Thus Leton, in a limited comparison of lecture and group discussion in a course in child development, found no differences that could be ascribed to the procedures used.[46]

A few studies attempted to appraise the effect of substituting group-led sessions for those which a teacher customarily leads. Based on studies in eleven departments at the University of Colorado, Hovey, Gruber, and Terrell found that the achievement of self-directed groups, meeting without an instructor for most scheduled sessions, was slightly superior, both at the course's conclusion and ten months later, to that of conventionally taught students; they also found that the experimental students were more curious. Yet the control students typically gave more favorable course evaluations—suggesting that students, like instructors, tend to resist the unfamiliar.[47] Other studies, confined typically to one or two courses, yielded similar findings. Scattered evidence also suggests that systematic training for student-led discussions improves these and general course achievement. But few studies have attempted to analyze the thought processes or verbal behavior of participants or even to identify major learning goals. It is not surprising that research findings under these circumstances are slim.

Independent Study. Provisions for independent study, both within and beyond regular courses, appear to be increasing. Felder, who examined practices in four-year colleges, found that two-thirds of the responding institutions currently had such provisions, and less than one-half of these were restricted to superior students.[48]

Antioch's carefully executed appraisal of independent study, reported by Churchill, showed that students in seven first-level general education courses who spent approximately one-half of the usual class time in independent study or small group meetings did as well and were as satisfied with the instructors and courses involved as were those who attended classes regularly. But all three methods produced little gain in "learning resourcefulness" or the achievement of skills and attitudes favoring continued independent study.[49]

In comparisons made in several colleges, involving the use of independent study procedures in a beginning psychology course, the conventionally taught students did slightly better than the experimental students on regular classroom tests, but McKeachie and others noted that the latter students developed a greater interest and sense of involvement in the subject matter.[50]

Although colleges are increasingly using off-campus learning experiences, research on their learning value is just beginning. Using chiefly student, faculty, and employer perceptions, Wilson and Lyons reported generally favorable conclusions from their appraisal of work-study plans in seventeen colleges.[51] Using information obtained from American students and from educators in the host countries, Weidner suggested that the better student-abroad programs have a substantial impact in the areas of general cultural values, political and international attitudes, and personal maturity.[52] Clearly there is fertile ground for research on these and other off-campus substitutes for conventional instruction.

Instructional Technology and Media. A remarkable feature of recent research on instructional technology and media is the swift change in emphasis from televised to programmed instruction. Lumsdaine and May provided an excellent guide to the extensive literature in this area,[53] much of which exists in mimeographed technical reports. Many reports of instructional media research conducted under the National Defense Education Act, Title VII, have been abstracted under the direction of W. H. Allen.[54]

Schramm's summary seemingly marks the end of the research

era in which massive comparisons were made between televised lectures and other teaching techniques. Of 100 studies at the college level, Schramm found three that favored television, thirteen that favored conventional instruction, and eighty-four that showed no significant differences in achievement. Attitudes of college students were sometimes negative but depended upon the subject, the teacher, and the type of viewer.[55]

In the Chicago City Junior College studies reported by Erickson and Chausow, television students, even those viewing at home, did as well as students in a face-to-face classroom setting. Student reaction to television was more favorable among home viewers and varied according to the subject of the course.[56] Janes found favorable attitudes toward televised instruction in a social science course to be positively related to length of viewing experience, intelligence, self-confidence, degree of authoritarianism, and course grade.[57]

Considerable interest has been shown recently in the use of television for special demonstration purposes. Evaluative studies, such as the one at Hunter College, have shown that televised demonstrations of classroom practices are as effective in teacher education as direct observation.[58] Similar uses were reported in other professional programs.

Although there seems to be general agreement that additional gross comparisons of televised and conventional teaching are unnecessary, no substantial alternative research strategy for instructional television has clearly emerged. One promising approach is illustrated by Siegel and Siegel, who are studying various ways to utilize television, taking account of different teaching objectives and different kinds of student viewers.[59] Another strategy, recommended by Lumsdaine and May, emphasizes the investigation of theoretically-relevant instructional variables.[60]

The past five years include almost the entire history of research on programmed instruction. Of 190 studies reported by Schramm, only twenty-five were made prior to 1960. Although many of these studies involved elementary and high school students, a significant proportion related to college-level instruction.[61]

As in research on television, comparisons of programmed

instruction and conventional instruction have been popular. Despite the limitations of such comparisons, it is interesting to note that, of college-level comparisons reviewed, approximately one-third favored programmed instruction and none favored conventional instruction.

Carpenter and Greenhill, who directed several representative studies at Pennsylvania State University, concluded that achievement in a mathematics and an English course was as good with programmed materials as with conventional instruction.[62] In a similar study, Ripple reported a significant advantage for programmed approaches in elementary psychology.[63] A common finding in such comparative studies is that instructional time is reduced when programmed materials are used.

Another kind of comparative study is illustrated by the work of Moore and Smith, who tested various ways of presenting the Holland-Skinner program in psychology, such as using machines or programmed texts, asking for written responses or merely having the material read, employing free-response or multiple-choice formats, and giving or not giving the student knowledge of results. As has been common in these studies, there were no significant differences on the criterion test between the various presentation groups.[64] Even when they presented the programs to groups by filmstrips or television, thereby eliminating the usual self-pacing features, Carpenter and Greenhill could find no difference in learning outcomes.[65] On the other hand, evidence exists that some ways of using programs may be more effective than others. Dick, for example, found an advantage when students studied programs in pairs rather than singly.[66]

Research on student reactions has been complicated by the great range in quality of programmed materials and the novelty of this approach. Robinson and Lerbinger reported generally favorable reactions to a programmed workbook which supplemented a Continental Classroom course.[67] But Banta, summarizing evaluations of the same program at different institutions, found that student reaction varied significantly from college to college.[68]

Despite the hope of psychologists that some problems of college teaching would readily be solved by programmed instruction, its contributions as revealed by research in this field are as yet quite modest. Perhaps its major value has been to stimulate clear specification of objectives and continuing revision of instructional materials on the basis of student learning. For some aspects of instruction at least, programs can save time for both instructor and student, with no apparent loss in learning.

As Lumsdaine and May report, research continues on the use of a variety of other audiovisual aids, including films and audiotapes.[69] In the college setting, particular emphasis has been given to evaluation of the language laboratory, which seems to offer definite advantages in foreign language programs stressing audiolingual skills. Scherer and Wertheimer, comparing two years of conventional instruction in German with instruction using an audiolingual method and language laboratory facilities, found that the latter produced superior speaking skills but inferior translating skills.[70]

The central contribution of research on instructional technology and media in this period has been to help television, programmed instruction, and language laboratories gain acceptance with college educators. A further task is to clarify how each of these can best be used in college instruction.

Student and Teacher Characteristics. The general climate for learning in a given college unquestionably affects student and instructor performance. However, no studies have systematically related this factor to the nature and quality of college instruction, and only occasional studies have explored the significance of student and teacher traits in influencing learning, even though these may account for much of the unexplained variance in achievement.

A few investigators who have related students' scholastic aptitude or prior knowledge to teaching method, have not identified any consistent patterns, though their findings suggest intriguing interactions among these variables.[71] In an important exploratory study of the influence of motivation on student learning, McKeachie found that the three motives investigated (affiliation, need for power, and achievement) interacted to some degree with teaching methods in influencing learning. Thus students who showed a strong affiliation motive did better in classes high in affiliative cues than in those with few such cues.[72] This research has been greatly extended in the Michigan Project, *Research on the Characteristics of Effective College Teaching.* A preliminary report confirmed the importance of motivational factors and other student traits in influencing instructional outcomes.[73]

Little has been determined, beyond what was reported in the late 1950's, regarding faculty members' personal characteristics and the meaning of these for their teaching. Getzels and Jackson succinctly summarized theories of personality and assessed existing instruments and research possibilities;[74] but in the period of this review only Corcoran and McKeachie, Isaacson, and Milholland examined specifically the characteristics of good and poor college teachers as seen by their students. Using an adapted version of Cattell's scales, Corcoran found that good teachers rate high in surgency (buoyancy and enthusiasm), comention (cultural interests), and cyclothymia (concern for people).[75] Similarly, McKeachie, Isaacson, and Milholland discovered that young teachers who were ranked high by their peers on surgency, culture, and emotional stability were the most likely to be viewed favorably by students.[76]

In another trail-blazing study, Solomon, Bezdek, and Rosenberg related eight factors, derived from reports by students and trained observers and actual tape recordings of teachers' behavior, to students' gains in factual knowledge and in comprehension.[77] Findings from this study suggest, as do those reported by McKeachie, Isaacson, and Milholland, that teaching styles do influence learning. But much more needs to be discovered about how teachers' personal traits influence their choice of methods and students' success and satisfactions in learning.

In general, recent studies of teaching methods and materials have, like their predecessors, yielded no clear-cut evidence of the superiority of any one approach. This situation unquestionably reflects problems in definition, design, and instrumentation; it also testifies to the strong common influence exerted by tradition and the competition for grades. Since students seem to acquire certain types of knowledge quite well on their own, teachers may properly stress skills of inquiry, interpretation, and application. And certainly innovations in teaching can be tried more boldly, without undue fear that standards of quality will be sacrificed.

NEXT STEPS IN RESEARCH

The major impression gained from a review of recent literature on college teachers and teaching is that research on these topics still claims far too little time, effort, and money. While a few excellent studies have emerged, educators lack carefully planned and cumulated research to guide decisions on staffing and instructional problems. Creative contributions made by isolated investigators need to be supplemented by campus-wide studies and by well mobilized regional and national efforts.

The start made in formulating theories of teaching should be vigorously continued in the years ahead. As theories are refined and effective ways are evolved to test them in college settings, they should contribute greatly to the improvement of teaching. The college faculty member, as well as the researcher, needs comprehensive and empirically supported theories to guide his efforts.

Progress charted recently in defining experimental variables also raises hope for the next decade of instructional research. Clearly, the many comparisons made using ambiguously defined experimental and control methods have added little to our knowledge of teaching and should not be continued. The experimental application of theoretically derived variables [78] constitutes one promising approach to such sharpened definition. Another attack, which Gage cogently supported [79] and which is well illustrated in the Solomon, Bezdek, and Rosenberg study, involves process-descriptive studies of teaching aimed at finding out what actually transpires in the classroom or laboratory. Further work along both these lines should aid in setting up meaningful experiments and in developing better theories of teaching.

Current concern for strengthening the subject content of college courses should also stimulate better studies of teaching. One reason research on teaching has been rather sterile is that it has often been considered in the abstract, without reference to the particular subject content involved. As more knowledge is gained about the structure of individual disciplines, both teaching methods and ways of evaluating their effectiveness may need rethinking.

Research patterns illustrated in some of the studies noted above also merit far wider application. More comprehensively planned studies will enable investigators to utilize a broad array of information on input, process, and output variables and to identify important interactions as well as main effects of the experimental variables. But, as Pullias counseled, preconceptions about acceptable methods of research should not restrict the investigator's vision.[80] A fresh idea tested in a limited way may promote excellence in teaching far more than a sophisticated study lacking such imagination.

Better ways also need to be found to diffuse research findings and to encourage trial of promising teaching methods and techniques. Since students as well as professors tend to resist change, established behaviors are not likely to be modified because an occasional faculty member tries a new approach. Without more effective means for stimulating experimentation and putting findings to productive use, many teachers will continue to cling jealously to methods developed in an earlier time.

Clearly, a much broader concept of research on staffing and teaching is needed. If today's pioneering efforts to test theoretical concepts and relationships under normal class conditions and to encompass the multiplicity of factors involved are to be extended, such research must receive high institutional priority. Only a strenuous, across-the-board effort holds promise for any major breakthrough on today's massive instructional problems.

NOTES

1. L. Wilson et al., *Studies of College Faculty* (Boulder, Colo.: Western Interstate Commission for Higher Education and the Study of Higher Education at Berkeley, 1961).

2. J. Adelson, "The Teacher as a Model," *The American College: A Psychological and Social Interpretation of the Higher Learning*, ed. N. S. Sanford (New York: John Wiley & Sons, 1962), pp. 396–417.

3. J. Katz, "Personality and Interpersonal Relations in the College Classroom," in Sanford, ed., *The American College,* pp. 365–95.

4. R. Knapp, "Changing Functions of the College Professor," in Sanford, ed., *The American College,* pp. 290–311.

5. J. W. Gustad, *The Career Decisions of College Teachers* (Atlanta, Ga.: Southern Regional Education Board, 1960).

6. R. E. Eckert and J. E. Stecklein, *Job Motivations and Satisfactions of College Teachers,* U. S. Department of Health, Education, and Welfare; Office of Education, Cooperative Research Monograph No. 7 (Washington: Government Printing Office, 1961).

7. E. W. Hartung, *Some Factors in the Choice of a Career in College Teaching of Biology* (Winchester, Mass.: New England Board of Higher Education, 1961).

8. N. Z. Medalia, *On Becoming a College Teacher: A Review of Three Variables,* Research Monograph No. 6 (Atlanta, Ga.: Southern Regional Education Board, 1963).

9. D. D. O'Dowd and D. C. Beardslee, "The Image of the College Professor," *American Association of University Professors Bulletin,* Vol. 47 (September, 1961), 216–21.

10. M. E. Corcoran, *Where Does College Teaching Stand in the Career Plans of Superior College Seniors?* (Minneapolis: Bureau of Institutional Research, University of Minnesota, 1961).

11. M. Kinnane, "Attitudes of College Students Toward College Teaching as a Career," *Educational Record,* Vol. 43 (April, 1962), 139–47.

12. B. Berelson, *Graduate Education in the United States* (New York: McGraw-Hill Book Co., 1960).

13. E. J. McGrath, *The Quantity and Quality of College Teachers,* Publication of the Institute of Higher Education (New York: Bureau of Publications, Teachers College, Columbia University, 1961).

14. Hartung, *College Teaching of Biology.*

15. D. Perkins and J. L. Snell, *The Education of Historians in the United States* (New York: McGraw-Hill Book Co., 1962).

16. J. C. Ewing and W. H. Stickler, "Progress in the Development of Higher Education as a Field of Professional Graduate Study and Research," *Journal of Teacher Education,* Vol. 15 (December, 1964), 397–403.

17. N. J. Tracy, "Orienting New Faculty Members in Colleges and Universities," *North Central Association Quarterly,* Vol. 36 (Fall, 1961), 214–21.

18. H. R. McCall, "Problems of New Faculty Members in Colleges and Universities," *North Central Association Quarterly,* Vol. 36 (Fall, 1961), 222–34.

19. J. W. Gustad, "Orientation and Faculty Development," *Educational Record,* Vol. 44 (July, 1963), 195–213.

20. L. A. Allen and R. L. Sutherland, *Role Conflicts and Congruences Experienced by New Faculty Members as They Enter the Culture of a College Community* (Austin, Texas: Hogg Foundation for Mental Health, 1963).

21. W. S. Miller and K. M. Wilson, *Faculty Development Procedures in Small Colleges: A Southern Survey,* Research Monograph No. 5 (Atlanta, Ga.: Southern Regional Education Board, 1963).

22. National Education Association, Research Division, *Teacher Supply and Demand in Universities, Colleges, and Junior Colleges, 1961–62 and 1962–63,* Research Report 1963–R3 (Washington: NEA, 1963); and NEA, Research Division, *Salaries Paid and Salary Practices in Universities, Colleges, and Junior Colleges, 1963–64,* Higher Education Series Research Report 1964–R3 (Washington: NEA, 1964).

23. R. E. Dunham and P. S. Wright, *Faculty and Other Professional Staff in Institutions of Higher Education, First Term 1961–62, Final Report,* U. S. Department of Health, Education, and Welfare; Office of Education, Circular No. 747 (Washington: Government Printing Office, 1964).

24. M. H. Ingraham and F. P. King, *The Outer Fringe: Faculty Benefits Other Than Annuities and Insurance* (Madison: University of Wisconsin Press, 1965).

25. J. Bernard, *Academic Women* (University Park: Pennsylvania State University Press, 1964).

26. See, for instance, H. Orlans, *The Effects of Federal Programs on Higher Education* (Washington: Brookings Institution, 1962).

27. J. E. Stecklein, *How to Measure Faculty Work Load* (Washington: American Council on Education, 1961).

28. J. Doi, "The Proper Use of Faculty Load Studies," *Studies of College Faculty,* Papers Presented at an Institute for College and University Administrators and Faculty, The University of California, Berkeley, 1961 (Boulder, Colo.: Western Interstate Commission for Higher Education, December, 1961), pp. 50–64.

29. J. W. Gustad, "Policies and Practices in Faculty Evaluation," *Educational Record,* Vol. 42 (July, 1961), 194–211.

30. Medalia, *Becoming a College Teacher.*

31. Gustad, *Career Decisions.*

32. J. E. Stecklein and R. L. Lathrop, *Faculty Attraction and Retention* (Minneapolis: Bureau of Institutional Research, University of Minnesota, 1960).

33. H. B. Sagen, "The Relationship of Certain Personality and Environmental Variables to the Satisfaction with Present Position of Faculty in Selected Liberal Arts Colleges" (unpublished Ph.D. dissertation, University of Minnesota, 1962); and Abstract in *Dissertation Abstracts,* Vol. 23, No. 9 (1963), 3241.

34. Allen and Sutherland, *Role Conflicts.*

35. N. L. Gage, ed., *Handbook of Research on Teaching* (Chicago: Rand McNally & Co., 1963).

36. National Society for the Study of Education, *Theories of Learning and Instruction,* Sixty-third Yearbook, Part 1 (Chicago: University of Chicago Press, 1964).

37. W. Hatch, ed., "New Dimensions in Higher Education," U. S. Department of Health, Education, and Welfare; Office of Education (Washington: Government Printing Office, 1960–65).

38. W. C. Eells, comp., *College Teachers and College Teaching: Second Supplement to the Annotated Bibliography Published in 1957* (Atlanta, Ga.: Southern Regional Education Board, 1962).

39. B. O. Smith, "A Concept of Teaching," *Language and Concepts in Education,* ed. Smith and R. H. Ennis (Chicago: Rand McNally & Co., 1961), pp. 86–101.

40. Gage, *Handbook,* Chapter 3.

41. D. P. Ausubel, *The Psychology of Meaningful Verbal Learning: An Introduction to School Learning* (New York: Grune & Stratton, 1963).

42. W. J. McKeachie, "Motivation, Teaching Methods, and College Learning," *Nebraska Symposium on Motivation, 1961,* Vol. 9 of *Current Theory and Research in Motivation,* ed. M. R. Jones (Lincoln: University of Nebraska Press, 1961), 111–42.

43. L. Siegel and L. C. Siegel, "The Instructional Gestalt: A Conceptual Framework and Design for Educational Research," *AV Communication Review,* Vol. 12 (Spring, 1964), 16–45.

44. See also W. J. McKeachie, R. L. Isaacson, and J. E. Milholland, *Research on the Characteristics of Effective College Teaching,* U. S. Department of Health, Education, and Welfare; Office of Education, Cooperative Research Project No. 850 (Ann Arbor: University of Michigan, 1964).

45. F. G. Macomber and L. Siegel, *Final Report of the Experimental Study in Instructional Procedures* (Oxford, Ohio: Miami University, 1960).

46. D. A. Leton, "An Evaluation of Course Methods in Teaching Child Development," *Journal of Educational Research,* Vol. 55 (November, 1961), 118–22.

47. D. E. Hovey, H. E. Gruber, and G. Terrell, "Effects of Self-Directed Study on Course Achievement, Retention, and Curiosity," *Journal of Educational Research,* Vol. 56 (March, 1963), 346–51.

48. D. Felder, "Independent-Study Practices in Colleges and Universities," *Journal of Higher Education,* Vol. 35 (June, 1964), 335–38.

49. R. D. Churchill, "Evaluation of Independent Study in College Courses" (unpublished Ph.D. dissertation, University of Minnesota, 1960); and Abstract in *Dissertation Abstracts,* Vol. 21, No. 7 (1961) 1841–42.

50. W. J. McKeachie *et al.,* "Individualized Teaching in Elementary Psychology," *Journal of Educational Psychology,* Vol. 51 (October, 1960), 285–91.

51. J. W. Wilson and E. H. Lyons, *Work-Study College Programs* (New York: Harper & Brothers, 1961).

52. E. W. Weidner, *The World Role of Universities* (New York: McGraw-Hill Book Co., 1962).

53. A. A. Lumsdaine and M. A. May, "Mass Communication and Educational Media," *Annual Review of Psychology,* ed. P. R. Farnsworth (Palo Alto, Calif.: Annual Reviews, Vol. 16 [1965]), 475–534.

54. W. H. Allen, ed., "Title VII Research Abstracts," *AV Communication Review,* 9: A1–A32, July–August, 1961; 9: A33–A58, November–December, 1961; 10: A61–A83, January–February, 1962; 10: A85–A120, May–June, 1962; 10: A122–A141, November–December, 1962; 11: A142–A172, September–October, 1963; 12: 109–26, Spring, 1964; 12: 233–55, Summer, 1964.

55. W. Schramm, "Learning from Instructional Television," *Review of Educational Research,* Vol. 32, No. 2 (April, 1962), 156–67.

56. C. G. Erickson and H. M. Chausow, *Chicago's TV College: Final Report of a Three Year Experiment of the Chicago City Junior College in Offering College Courses for Credit via Open Circuit Television* (Chicago: Chicago City Junior College, 1960).

57. R. W. Janes, "Preexisting Attitudes of College Students to Instructional Television," *AV Communication Review,* Vol. 12 (Fall, 1964), 325–36.

58. N. Stoller, G. S. Lesser, and P. I. Freedman, "A Comparison

of Methods of Observation in Preservice Teacher Training," *AV Communication Review,* Vol. 12 (Summer, 1964), 177–97.

59. Siegel and Siegel, *AV Communication Review,* Vol. 12, 16–45.

60. Lumsdaine and May, *Annual Review of Psychology,* Vol. 16, 475–534.

61. W. Schramm, *The Research on Programed Instruction—An Annotated Bibliography,* U. S. Department of Health, Education, and Welfare; Office of Education, Bulletin 1964, No. 35 (Washington: Government Printing Office, 1964).

62. C. R. Carpenter and L. P. Greenhill, *Comparative Research on Methods and Media for Presenting Programed Courses in Mathematics and English* (University Park: Pennsylvania State University Press, 1963).

63. R. E. Ripple, "Comparison of the Effectiveness of a Programed Text with Three Other Methods of Presentation," *Psychological Reports,* Vol. 12 (February, 1963), 227–37.

64. J. W. Moore and W. I. Smith, "The Role of Knowledge of Results in Programed Instruction," *Psychological Reports,* Vol. 14 (April, 1964), 407–23.

65. Carpenter and Greenhill, *Comparative Research.*

66. W. Dick, "Retention as a Function of Paired and Individual Use of Programed Instruction," *Journal of Programed Instruction,* Vol. 2 (Fall, 1963), 17–23.

67. E. J. Robinson and O. Lerbinger, "Subjective Reactions of Students to a Programed Workbook for a Continental Classroom Course," *AV Communication Review,* Vol. 11 (November–December, 1963), 241–52.

68. T. J. Banta, "Attitudes Toward a Programed Text: 'The Analysis of Behavior' Compared with 'A Textbook on Psychology,' " *AV Communication Review,* Vol. 11 (November–December, 1963), 227–40.

69. Lumsdaine and May, *Annual Review of Psychology,* Vol. 16, 475–534.

70. G. A. C. Scherer and M. Wertheimer, *A Psycholinguistic Experiment in Foreign-Language Teaching* (New York: McGraw-Hill Book Co., 1964).

71. H. E. Gruber and M. Weitman, "The Growth of Self-Reliance," *School and Society,* Vol. 91 (May 4, 1963), 222–23; also see Siegel and Siegel, *AV Communication Review,* Vol. 12, 16–45.

72. McKeachie, *Nebraska Symposium.*

73. McKeachie, Isaacson, and Milholland, *Effective College Teaching.*

74. J. W. Getzels and P. W. Jackson, "The Teacher's Personality and Characteristics," in Gage, ed., *Handbook,* pp. 506–82.

75. Corcoran, *Career Plans of Superior College Seniors.*

76. McKeachie, Isaacson, and Milholland, *Effective College Teaching.*

77. D. Solomon, W. E. Bezdek, and L. Rosenberg, *Teaching Styles and Learning* (Chicago: Center for the Study of Liberal Education for Adults, 1963).

78. See Lumsdaine and May, *Annual Review of Psychology,* Vol. 16, 475–534, and McKeachie, Isaacson, and Milholland, *Effective College and Teaching.*

79. N. L. Gage, "The Appraisal of College Teaching: An Analysis of Ends and Means," *Journal of Higher Education,* Vol. 32 (January, 1961), 17–22.

80. E. V. Pullias, "Factors Influencing Excellence in College and University Teaching," *Educational Record,* Vol. 44 (July, 1963), 243–47.

8

FIVE COLLEGE
ENVIRONMENTS

C. Robert Pace

C. Robert Pace began his investigations of campus "climates" while
at Syracuse University. One of the most productive investigators in
that field, he has been Professor of Higher Education at the University
of California at Los Angeles since 1961.

The research described in this article concerns identifying the educationally and psychologically functional environment of a college. Cumulatively, rules and regulations, personnel policies, classroom practices, activities and interests of students and staff, features and facilities, and so on, constitute an
educational press upon the awareness of students and hence
psychologically tend to make some kinds of behavior more
satisfying and rewarding than others in the particular environment. The press of the environment, as the student sees it,
defines what he must cope with and clarifies for him the direction his behavior must take if he is to find satisfaction and
reward within the dominant culture of the college. The environmental press, in this sense, is closely related to the concept of
objectives—for it suggests the implicit or operational influences
of the college, whether or not these agree with the explicitly
stated purposes.

An instrument based on this concept is the College Characteristics Index, now in its third revision.[1] It consists of 300
statements about college life. The statements refer to curriculum, to college teaching and classroom activities, to rules and
regulations and policies, to student organizations and activities
and interests, to features of the campus, etc.

Some of the items are quite objective in that they refer to easily observable or verifiable events or practices or features of the colleges. For example: "There are no fraternities or sororities. Professors usually take attendance in class. Concerts and art exhibits always draw big crowds of students. Students' midterm and final grades are reported to parents." Other items are rather subjective or impressionistic. For example: "Many students here develop a strong sense of responsibility about their role in contemporary social and political life. Everyone has a lot of fun at this school. Modern art and music get little attention here. Students set high standards of achievement for themselves." These examples show briefly what the content of the test is like.

Structurally, the items are grouped into thirty scales of ten items each, these being environmental press counterparts of thirty personality needs taken originally from Henry Murray's classification,[2] and included in the Activities Index by George Stern. There are, for example, scales to measure the press toward Understanding, Reflectiveness, Objectivity, Nurturance, Succorance, Affiliation, Order, Deference, Energy, Change, Sentience.

The items themselves are answered by college students— TRUE if they think the statement is generally characteristic of their college, is something which occurs or might occur, is the way people tend to feel or act; and FALSE if they think the statement is generally not characteristic of the college.

So far, the Index has been tried out in nearly 100 colleges and universities. Enough is known about the test itself to say with some confidence that it is psychometrically adequate. A brief accounting will serve to verify this statement.

(1) Seventy-nine per cent of the test items have a discrimination index of .40 or higher, and ninety-nine per cent have a discrimination index of .20 or higher.

(2) The variance of scores within institutions is significantly smaller than the variance of scores between institutions.

(3) What students say is true or false about the college environment is not influenced by their own personality

needs. The College Index is not, in other words, a personality test in disguise.[3]

(4) There is as much agreement in responses to the so-called subjective or impressionistic items as there is to the items which are more readily verifiable.[4]

(5) The overall picture of the college environment obtained from responses of faculty members and administrators to the test is highly consistent with the picture obtained from student responses.

(6) The results obtained from small, highly selected top scholarship students are very consistent with results obtained from a larger and representative cross section of students.

(7) Test-retest results from the same students are highly consistent.

All these correlations, between students and faculty, between representative and unrepresentative samples, between descriptions taken several months apart, are around .90.

From the accumulated test results, what can be learned about the variety of college cultures in America, about the extent to which colleges differ from one another in their presumed psychological impact upon students, and about the variables which tend to go together in defining the psychological characteristics of colleges?

In the spring of 1959 groups of students in some sixty institutions filled out the College Characteristics Index. Out of this testing program, thirty-two institutions were selected as a normative sample, consisting of liberal arts colleges (highly selective and relatively unselective, nonsectarian and denominational, coeducational and noncoeducational), universities (public and private), and various professional schools (education, engineering, and business, some separate and some parts of larger universities). There are some notable omissions in this norm group—none from the Ivy League and none from the West Coast—but it is nevertheless a diverse assortment of institutions spread geographically over most of the country.

How different are these institutions?[5] One simple way to

answer this question is to see whether the features most characteristic of one college are also most characteristic of another. The test yields scores for 30 variables or features. These 30 scores, expressed as standard scores, can be arranged in rank order from high to low. By comparing the rank order of scores between colleges, one gets a general index of the degree of similarity between one environment and another. For the 32 institutions these rank order correlations ranged from +.93 to −.87. Among some colleges the relative environmental pressures are nearly identical; among others the relative pressures are almost totally opposite.

If all one knows about the institution is that it is a small denominational liberal arts college, or a large state university, or an engineering school, or a teacher training school, or that it is located in a particular geographic region, one knows very little about its psychological environment. Familiar classification systems cover up a great diversity. The correlations among seven liberal arts colleges, all private and nonsectarian, ranged from +.93 to +.01. Among seven small liberal arts denominational colleges the correlations ranged from +.78 to −.35. Among seven large universities, both public and private, they ranged from +.87 to −.13; among three teacher training schools, from +.71 to −.35; among four engineering schools, from +.64 to +.10. Six institutions located in southeastern states ranged from +.82 to −.75. The correlations among four New England colleges ranged from +.72 to −.80. These are extraordinary differences.

If one looks instead at relationships among the test variables (environmental press scores) across the normative group of 32 colleges and universities, one sees the college environments in a different perspective. This view reveals what kinds of pressures or characteristics tend to go together in college environments generally, and how the presence or absence of one group of characteristics is related to the presence or absence of others.

Two major factors [6] apparently account for most of the differences among college environments. One is intellectual; the other is social. The intellectual dimension runs from a high stress on abstract, theoretical, scholarly understanding to a high stress on practical, status-oriented concerns. The social dimension runs from a high stress on group welfare to a rebellion against group life. It is possible, further, to differentiate two patterns of high intellectual emphasis—one humanistic and one scientific. Tentatively, then, five clusters, or types of environments, can be described.

The first type of environment is identified by high scores on the environmental press scales for Humanism, Reflectiveness, Sentience, Understanding, Objectivity, Energy, and Achievement. Here are some of the items characterizing this pattern of press:

> The school offers many opportunities for students to understand and criticize important works in art, music, and drama. A lecture by an outstanding literary critic would be well attended. Books dealing with psychological problems or personal values are widely read and discussed. Long, serious, intellectual discussions are common among the students. On nice days many classes meet outdoors on the lawn. Concerts and art exhibits always draw big crowds of students. There is a lot of emphasis on preparing for graduate work. Many students are interested in round tables, panel meetings, or other formal discussions. The school has an excellent reputation for academic freedom. Class discussions are typically vigorous and intense. The professors really push the students' capacities to the limit. Students set high standards of achievement for themselves. Faculty members put a lot of energy and enthusiasm into their teaching.

These are environmental characteristics which encourage curiosity about new knowledge and new ideas, self-understanding, new sensations and appreciations. College is an expanding experience, testing the limits of one's capacities.

The second type of environment is also strongly intellectual and energetic, but its predominant emphasis is toward science and competition for achievement. It is identified by high scores on the press scales for Scientism, Change, Fantasied Achievement, and by low scores on the press scales for Adaptiveness [7] and Order. Here are some characteristic features:

> Laboratory facilities in the natural sciences are excellent. Many of the science professors are actively engaged in research. When students get together they often talk about science. The students represent a great variety in nationality, religion, and social status. The history and traditions of the college are not emphasized. Most students do not dress and act very much alike. The faculty encourage students to think about exciting and unusual careers. Student organizations are not closely supervised. Professors do not regularly check up on the students to make sure that assignments are being carried out properly and on time. Professors do not usually take attendance. Classes do not always meet at their regularly scheduled time and place.

The environment appears to be one in which survival is the students' responsibility. The curriculum is there. The laboratories are good. The professors are busy with research. If the student wants to learn science, let him learn it. There are exciting rewards for those who have the ability and the independent motivation to survive the competition.

The third type of environment is quite the opposite of the two which have been described. The dominant concern in the third type is with the practical and applied rather than the abstract or theoretical; and with this goes an equally strong concern for establishing one's status in relation to peers and accepting one's status in relation to authority. The scales which go together in this cluster are Practicality, Abasement, Dominance, Play, and Sex. Items descriptive of this kind of environment are as follows:

> The college offers many really practical courses such as typing, report writing, etc. Most students are interested in careers in business, engineering, management, and other practical affairs. Students are more interested in specialization than in general liberal education. Students are not encouraged to criticize administrative policies and teaching

practices. For a period of time freshmen have to take orders from upperclassmen. There is a lot of apple-polishing around here. Student elections generate a lot of intense campaigning and strong feeling. There is a recognized group of student leaders on this campus. There are lots of dances, parties, and social activities. Every year there are carnivals, parades, and other festive events on the campus. There is a lot of informal dating during the week—at the library, snack bar, movies, etc. There are several popular spots where a crowd of boys and girls can always be found.

One may wonder why the scales labeled Play and Sex belong in this cluster. The reason is that many of the items in these scales reflect the importance attached to establishing interpersonal status and to gaining privilege and prestige in the campus community.

The fourth type of environment is identified by high scores on the press scales for Affiliation, Nurturance, Succorance, and Conjunctivity. The emphasis is on human relations, group welfare, social responsibility, and the well-mannered and well-managed community. Here are some of the items characterizing this type of environment:

The school helps everyone get acquainted. There is a lot of group spirit. Faculty members call students by their first names. Many upperclassmen play an active role in helping new students adjust to campus life. The college regards training people for service to the community as one of its major responsibilities. The school has a reputation for being very friendly. Students often help one another with their lessons. Counseling and guidance services are really personal, patient, and extensive. Instructors clearly explain the goals and purposes of their courses. Assignments are usually clear and specific, making it easy for students to plan their studies effectively. Activities in most student organizations are carefully and clearly planned.

The fifth and last cluster is best described as a rebellion against the group-welfare-oriented community. The high press scales here are Aggression and Impulsion. The following items are illustrative:

> Students are sometimes noisy and inattentive at concerts or lectures. Many students seem to expect other people to adapt to them rather than trying to adapt themselves to others. Students occasionally plot some sort of escapade or rebellion. Many informal student activities are unplanned and spontaneous. There seems to be a jumble of papers and books in most faculty offices. Students often start projects without trying to decide in advance how they will develop or where they may end.

Here then are five ways of characterizing college environments. The first is predominantly humanistic, reflective, and sentient. College is an expanding intellectual experience, testing the limits of curiosity about new ideas, new sensations, new capacities, and self-understanding. The second, equally demanding and vigorous, is predominantly scientific and competitive, requiring a high degree of individual concentration for survival. The third is practical, applied, concerned with interpersonal and extrapersonal status; in the pursuit of utilitarian goals, one's relationship to authority and the gaining of privileges and visible rewards are important. The fourth type of environment is strongly other-directed. There is a high level of concern for group welfare, friendships, organization, and social responsibility. The fifth type is aggressive and impulsive, in rebellion chiefly against the other-directed, highly socialized community.

The relationships between these five patterns of college environment variables should be of particular interest to college administrators, personnel officers, and faculty members. Table 1 shows the correlations.

The variables which push toward intellectual expansion and achievement, whether humanistic or scientific, correlate positively among themselves and negatively with the practical, status-oriented variables. The humanistic emphasis is unrelated to the group welfare emphasis and unrelated to rebelliousness. Apparently the strongly science-oriented environment is also characterized by nonconformity and independence. The status-oriented, practical environment has some positive relationship to rebellion but little or no relationship to group welfare. It is clearly anti-intellectual but not anti-knowledge. The college as a friendly, socializing, well-mannered environment is not anti-intellectual in general, but it is anti-scientific and competitive, and anti-rebellious.

Personnel practices, rules and regulations, teaching methods, study requirements, features and facilities, and the whole network of events and activities and relationships to be found on a college campus, constitute a system of pressures or influences which define the psychological educational character of the environment. The various pieces of the college environment fit together (at least tentatively they seem to) in the five broad patterns just described.

TABLE 1

AVERAGE CORRELATIONS BETWEEN CLUSTERS OF VARIABLES

	Human-istic	Scientific	Prac-tical, Status	Human Relations	Rebel-lious-ness
Humanistic, reflective, sentient	.75				
Scientific, competitive	.48	.55			
Practical, status-oriented	−.64	−.41	.67		
Human relations, group welfare	−.01	−.45	.12	.54	
Rebelliousness	−.08	.26	.23	−.37	.66

One can now re-look at colleges to see whether these patterns are, in fact, exemplified in the environment of real institutions. For this purpose a factor analysis of institutions was made. A cluster of institutions emerged at each end of the principal axis; and at a right angle from the center of this axis was another cluster of institutions. By referring to the press scores of each institution in these three clusters, one finds that the groups can be described as high intellectual, high practical, and high social. These obviously correspond to the major clusters which emerged when the variables, rather than the institutions, were analyzed—humanistic, scientific, practical, status-oriented, and group-welfare-oriented. The patterns of environmental press found across a heterogeneous assortment of colleges are also found clearly within the environment of individual colleges, as Figure 1 illustrates. The bars show the range of standard score

FIGURE 1

PATTERNS OF PRESS IN THREE TYPES OF COLLEGES

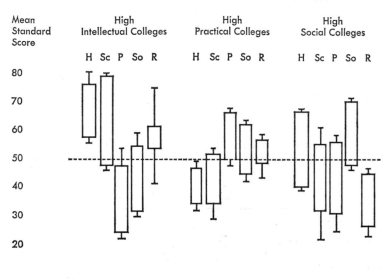

Legend: Standard Scores:

    H = Humanistic variables   Mean = 50
    Sc = Scientific variables   Sigma = 20
    P = Practical, status-oriented variables
    So = Social, group welfare variables
    R = Rebellion variables

means for all colleges in each group on all the variables in each press cluster, with the one highest and the one lowest mean score indicated by the thin line extensions on the bars.

Among the high intellectual institutions, all the standard score means on all seven humanistic variables rank higher than all the standard score means on all five of the practical, status-oriented variables. There is no overlap. The chart shows many other examples of non-overlapping distributions. In general, the relationships presented in the correlation table are clearly illustrated in the chart.

A few not-too-cautious speculations about the meaning of these results may be provocative. Environmental differences between colleges may be greater than individual differences between students. Certainly no one type of college environment will serve all types of students. What types of students will profit most in what types of environments is the next question on the research agenda. And for the larger and more complex colleges and universities, one also needs to raise this question about subcultures which operate within the general environment. Meanwhile, one might suppose that the friendly, social, group-welfare kind of environment would be good for future dwellers in suburbia and the employees and managers of industries that are self-conscious about human relations. It may be especially relevant for women. Togetherness is an important and respectable virtue; but in the economic, cultural, and political diversity of the modern world, socialization is not enough. It is a useful process; but what ends shall this happy family pursue? The rebellion environment, on the other hand, merely reacts against socialization and offers no substitute direction of its own. The practical, status-oriented environment doubtless provides needed skills for society's work; and for some it may offer practice in the struggle for room at the top. For most, it seems more likely to be a good influence in maintaining a *status quo* of ideas and human relations; and in this sense it can be called a containment environment. For the bright and adventurous, the intellectual-humanistic-scientific environment is full of promise and excitement. It may be annoyingly rebellious at times for the administrator, and it may not have much good neighborly spirit in it, but it is potentially creative. It offers the hope of an adolescent breakthrough toward new directions, new solutions, and new ways of life.

POSTSCRIPT 1968

In the years subsequent to original publication of this article, the writer has developed a modified and restructured set of measures for describing the college environment. The revised instrument, called College and University Environment Scales (CUES), is published and distributed by Educational Testing Service, Princeton, New Jersey. CUES consist of 150 of the original 300 items, selected to describe more efficiently and more simply the major dimensions along which college environments differ from one another. The 150 items form five scales of 30 items each. These scales, or dimensions, are labeled Scholarship, Awareness, Community, Propriety, and Practicality. They generally resemble the five college environments described in the 1960 article. The Scholarship scale reflects an emphasis on competitively high academic achievement and a serious interest in knowledge and theories. The Awareness scale reflects an emphasis on the arts, on personal meaning, and on concern about the world and the present and future condition of mankind. The Community scale describes a friendly, cohesive, group-oriented campus. The Practicality scale suggests an instrumental, entrepreneurial, and bureaucratic environmental press. Finally, the Propriety scale suggests a polite, considerate environment, as opposed to one that is demonstrative, unconventional, and rebellious.

CUES are scored after the fashion of a public opinion poll. When students agree, by a majority of two to one or greater, that a statement is generally true about their campus, that statement is regarded as "characteristic" of the environment. The score on each scale is simply the number of statements (from zero to 30) answered in the keyed direction by 66 per cent or more of the student reporters—that is, by a consensus of two to one or greater. Interpretive norms are based on a cross-section of fifty colleges and universities.

To date, more than 300 colleges and universities have used CUES. At the present time, data from a new national norm group of 100 universities are being analyzed and will be reported, together with the results of numerous research studies, in a revised and enlarged manual for CUES.

Meanwhile, the most complete information about CUES appears in the *Technical Manual*. This and other references to studies of college environments are listed chronologically below:

Pace, C. R. and A. McFee. "The College Environment," *Review of Educational Research,* October, 1960, 311–20.

Pace, C. R. "Methods of Describing College Cultures," *Teachers College Record,* January, 1962, 267–77.

Pace, C. R. *College and University Environment Scales: Technical Manual.* Princeton, New Jersey: Educational Testing Service, 1963.

Michael, W. and E. Boyer. "Campus Environment," *Review of Educational Research,* October, 1965, 264–76.

Pace, C. R. "When Students Judge Their College," *College Board Review,* Winter, 1965–66, 26–28.

Pace, C. R. "Selective Higher Education for Diverse Students," *Universal Higher Education,* ed. E. J. McGrath New York: McGraw-Hill, 1966, pp. 159–73.

Pace, C. R. "Perspectives on the Student and His College," *The Student and the College,* ed. L. Dennis and Joseph Kauffman. Washington, D. C.: American Council on Education, 1966, pp. 76–100.

NOTES

1. The College Characteristics Index was developed jointly by the writer and George G. Stern at Syracuse University. For the rationale of the test, together with some early results, see: C. Robert Pace and George G. Stern, "An Approach to the Measurement of Psychological Characteristics of College Environments," *Journal of Educational Psychology,* Vol. 49, No. 5 (October, 1958), 269–77.

2. H. A. Murray, *Explorations in Personality* (New York: Oxford University Press, 1938).

3. A detailed analysis is reported in Anne McFee, "The Relation of Selected Factors to Student Perception of a College Environment" (unpublished Master's thesis, Syracuse University, Syracuse, N. Y., 1959).

4. *Ibid.*

5. The analyses presented in the remainder of this article were made jointly by the writer and Anne McFee at the Center for Advanced Study in the Behavioral Sciences, Stanford, California.

6. This observation is based on a very simple factor analysis (centroid program for IBM 650 computer) with one rotation of the first factor. The correlation matrix was developed from the standard score means on each of the 30 variables (converted to rank orders) for each of the 32 schools in the norm group.

7. A better name for the Adaptiveness scale would be Closeness of Supervision.

9

THE IMPACT OF HIGHER EDUCATION ON STUDENT ATTITUDES, VALUES, AND CRITICAL THINKING ABILITIES

Paul L. Dressel and Irvin J. Lehmann

A member of the faculty in psychology at Michigan State University since 1934, Paul Dressel has been Director of Institutional Research since 1959 and Assistant Provost since 1960. He has published extensively in his chief areas of interest—measurement and evaluation in higher education.

Irvin J. Lehmann is Associate Professor in Evaluation Services in the University College of Michigan State University.

In 1957, Philip Jacob started a continuing controversy about the impact of higher education on student values by systematically reviewing a wide range of data from unrelated research projects and interpreting them to indicate that:

(1) "the impetus to change does not come from the formal educational process";

(2) students are "unabashedly self-centered" and greatly value the "material" aspects of life;

(3) colleges produced no great changes in values, but increased conformity—"more homogeneity and greater consistency of values among students at the end of their four years than when they begin." [1]

Jacob's statements were variously viewed as unjustified (by social scientists who criticized his basic sources and methodology); as irrationally cynical (by administrators convinced that the major contribution of colleges resides in their molding of youthful lives around time-tested values); and with indifference (by the large majority of college teachers who view their responsibility as limited to the inculcation of factual knowledge).

Jacob, of course, was not the first researcher in this area. Most previous researchers, however, focused their attention on *specific changes* in student attitudes and opinions about current social, religious, economic, or political issues.[2] Many studies, too, had been concerned with limited personality characteristics, such as authoritarianism, ethnocentrism, rigidity, and so on. Most of these investigations were cross-sectional rather than longitudinal, and few involved large numbers of students. On the whole, such restricted studies contributed little to the understanding of the impact of the four-year college experience on the student.

A few studies of the total impact of college have been carried out in relatively small, selective colleges, such as Vassar, Bennington, and Sarah Lawrence. These more inclusive studies have focused attention on the need to study the student's total environmental matrix in attempting to determine and explain changes in attitudes and values. Comprehensive reviews in this area are *The Impact of College*, by Freedman, and *The American College*, edited by Sanford. In his brief survey, Freedman has highlighted the important research reports, including those with controversial results. Reporting upon the longitudinal study at Vassar College, Freedman concluded that substantial personality changes occur between the time the student enters as a freshman and when she leaves college four years later. (Seniors tend to be more mature but less stable: they tend to be less "feminine"; they are less authoritarian, more tolerant, and display greater religious liberalism; they demonstrate greater acceptance of intellectual values and greater internal conflict than freshmen.) [3]

In a chapter of *The American College*, Webster, Freedman, and Heist discuss in a most illuminating manner the problem of change in students' attitudes and values. Reviewing studies conducted before World War II, the authors conclude that "in general, students in college changed in the direction of greater liberalism and sophistication in their political, social, and religious outlooks." They report similar trends evident in their subsequent research on college student populations.[4]

The part played by the "campus climate" in changing attitudes and values of college students is explored in the work of Eddy [5] and that of Brown and Bystrym.[6] Eddy feels that "perhaps the best way to transmit values is to create an 'atmosphere' on the campus." By visitation and interview of faculty, administrators, and students at twenty colleges and universities of various types throughout the United States, Eddy found that experiences outside the classroom were a factor of paramount significance in the development of *character*, and that particular aspects of the environment, such as attitudes, surroundings, extra activities, manners, and morals, have the power either to reinforce or to negate all that the college has to offer. Furthermore, he contends that "the best environment for the development of character is the result of unity in common goals, a communicated tradition to which all phases of campus life make their particular contribution."

Eddy found further that the "level of expectancy" in all matters concerning and involving the student in the college environment is a highly important determinant of *what happens* to him. The level of expectancy controls not just academic situations but social relationships, group life, and, in fact, all that happens to the student. He concluded, again, that "the level (of expectancy) is established most successfully in the acceptance by all of a common task, a common goal. It is reached only by the mutual assumption of particular responsibilities. Beyond what the college expects of itself, it must maintain a high but realistic level of expectations of its faculty." [7]

In summary, results of both longitudinal and cross-sectional studies of college students demonstrate that significant changes in the attitudes, values, interests, and beliefs of college students do occur between the freshman and senior years. Very little evidence exists, however, that any one factor from the multitude of college experiences explains changes in attitudes and values. Changes in personality characteristics during school and college years may be a function of the person's maturity or personality, a function of "the times we live in," the direct result of college experiences, or a combination of two or more such factors.[8]

Individuals adopt only those attitudes and values which will help them achieve desired ends [9] and which are normally sanctioned by the community in which they live.[10] In addition, the extent to which attitudes and values are modifiable depends upon the nature of the modifying experience,[11] the type of contact,[12] the personality make-up of the individual,[13] the group's approval of new attitudes,[14] and the subject's perception of the outcome.[15] Because of the continual interaction of these variables, it is difficult indeed to conclude, as did Jacob, that neither courses, nor instructors, nor instructional methods have a marked impact upon student values.[16]

Holding our conclusions in abeyance for the moment, however, we may agree with Raushenbush:

> If student mores and the influence of the peer group and the experiences outside the classroom are as important as all this research has indicated, the conclusion we should come to is, not the pessimistic one that education does not matter at all, but rather that education has another job to do, perhaps beyond the one educators have felt was their job. Colleges must take responsibility for creating a *climate of values* that will give some direction to student mores.[17] [Emphasis supplied.]

THE MICHIGAN STATE UNIVERSITY STUDY

The prior research, briefly and inadequately reviewed in the previous paragraphs, left us with the confused impression that college students do change, but that no one knows quite how, or why. The studies available, limited in numbers and types of institutions, lacked meaning for a large, complex university. The tendency to divorce attitudes and values from development of critical thinking abilities seemed, too, to savor of interest in changes wrought through indoctrination or unconscious assimilation of values, rather than through conscious modification by the student as a result of forthright consideration of the implications of espousal of alternative values. Moreover, the fact of change in college-going students does not establish the role of the college as effector of the change.

Although comparison of changes in values of college-going and non-college-going youth presents—because of the selective factors involved in college attendance—insurmountable difficulties, it seemed to us that some of the deficiencies of most studies could be reduced by noting changes *at intervals* over the four college years, and by comparing changes of those remaining for the full four years with changes in those individuals withdrawing from college after varying lengths of stay. Finally, we felt that, by judicious combination of objective evidence from a number of instruments—including a test of critical thinking, a number of questionnaires developed specifically in relation to student experiences and student phraseology, and interview materials from both students and faculty—a more student-oriented assessment of changes and probable effecting factors might be possible.

We wanted to learn something of the *degree* and *direction* of change in critical thinking, in attitudes, and in values at various stages of progress through college; and having done this, to compare the changes over a four-year span for those individuals completing a degree with those who withdrew at various stages. We were unwilling to delimit the study to any particular set of values deemed *a priori* desirable, although we were inclined to expect that the majority of the student population would improve in critical thinking, and would become less stereotypic in beliefs and more receptive to new ideas.

From previous studies, we concluded that sex, religious beliefs, socio-economic backgrounds, courses, instruction, the gamut of college-related experiences, and maturation would all be influential factors in determining the nature and extent of changes in individuals.

From these admitted preconceptions flowed many specific questions to be investigated and many hypotheses to be tested. The range and types of data are suggested by the list of data collection instruments and procedures used:

Major battery:
   Test of Critical Thinking, Form G
   Inventory of Beliefs, Form I
   Prince's Differential Values Inventory
   Rokeach's Dogmatism Scale
   College Objectives Checklist (locally developed)
   College Qualification Test (Psychological Corporation)
   MSU Reading Test
   MSU English Test
   Experience Inventories, I and II (locally developed)

Minor battery:
   Allport-Vernon-Lindzey Study of Values
   Wesley's Rigidity Scale
   Sophomore and junior year interviews
   Interviews with academic personnel

It was not possible to accumulate all of this information on all students, but initial testing of freshmen and repetition at the end of the freshman year and at the end of the senior year were nearly complete on the first five items of the major battery. Other instruments and procedures were used, with samples so chosen as to be reasonably representative of the total student body. Discontinuing students were asked by mail to take a reduced set of tests and to return questionnaires that had been so selected as to permit comparisons with those students who were surveyed in more detail. The cooperation of two small liberal arts colleges in administering many of the instruments in a pattern paralleling that at Michigan State University was also obtained. The study involved nearly 3,000 freshmen initially, repetitions of data collection with groups of from 500 to 1,000, and follow-up data from over 600 withdrawals. In sheer numbers of individuals involved and range of information collected, this study is very likely the most extensive one of its kind carried on by any single institution. Analyses of the data included variance and covariance analyses, multiple discriminant function analyses, factor analyses, content analyses, and various subjective judgmental assessments. In recording these facts, the intent is not to claim perfection in design, data collection, or analytical procedures; rather, it is to say that the findings reported here are based upon a comprehensive program of research.

OBSERVATIONS AND REFLECTIONS GENERATED BY THE STUDY

One obvious problem in such a comprehensive project was that of analyzing and interpreting the massive accumulation of data. Possible interrelationships were too numerous to pursue exhaustively. Problems of terminology and definition continually beset us in attempting to interpret seemingly inconsistent results and in stating conclusions in an objective manner. To what extent, for example, are stereotypy, rigidity, and dogmatism really distinct? Can one use such terms without making, or at least appearing to make, some value judgment regarding them? For whom are "traditional" values traditional? Are apparent changes really changes, or simply a result of increased sophistication and precision in interpretation of words and statements? With students who have not consciously confronted and assessed their attitudes and values, can inventories or interviews get at their convictions?

There is a great diversity in the experiences of students in a large university, and perhaps even greater diversity in the extent of personal involvement in and reaction to any given experience. Instructors with no recollection of contact with certain students were credited as having marked impact on the attitudes and values of these students. Some students, apparently, are attracted only to teachers and to student associates whose attitudes and values correspond closely to their own and, in them, consequently, they find reinforcement rather than incentive for self-examination and change.

Violently contrasting views are current among both students and faculty as to the responsibility of a college for promoting changes in attitudes and values. In interviews, numerous students expressed resentment at the implication that their basic beliefs and values would in any way be influenced by their college experiences. Instructors, interviewed to ascertain their intent and their observations in respect to value change, often disavowed any interest in or concern for such change. Thus, the study seemed to be seeking value changes in a milieu in which conscious concern for value change was disavowed by all parties!

Although higher education seems obviously committed to exposing students to some set of broad (though not always clearly expressed) values, the assumption of many of the faculty members and students seemed to be that presence in an institution involves an *a priori* acceptance of these values rather than participation in a planned program of experiences which highlight and possibly encourage assimilation of these values.

Very different views also exist about what changes in attitudes and values are desirable. When evidence accrued that many seniors, though not necessarily less religious than they were as freshmen, no longer accepted specific tenets or dogmas of their particular church affiliation, it was repeatedly pointed out that such a finding should be reported with great discretion, since it would be construed by some groups as evidence that college experiences were deleterious rather than constructive. Similarly, many students, as seniors, viewed the vocational significance of a college education as much less important than the acquiring of a broad liberal education. Such a finding is simply not accepted by some vocationally oriented segments of the faculty, who aspire to increase vocationally oriented education at the expense of the liberal. In some cases, such adverse reactions or doubts may lead to the accusation that the investigator, either by unconscious bias or malicious intent, forced the unhappy finding.

College attendance commonly involves some weakening of the dependence of youth on home and parents, and is paralleled for the non-college-attending youth by acceptance of full-time employment. Thus, the years immediately following completion of secondary school are closely related to the assumption by youth of a greater degree of freedom and responsibility—a heady and maturing experience. How much, then, of any change which takes place during the college years is really a result of college experiences, and how much is a result simply of the freedom to question and doubt values imposed by parents and the home community? The college should not claim credit for, nor should it be blamed for, changes which are a normal part of the maturation process. As our report of findings will indicate, we found the distinction not an easy one to make. Plant had previously hypothesized that the function of a college is simply to accelerate the process of change already in operation in the society at large.[18] Even this hypothesis, on closer examination, involves the highly debatable issue of whether higher education should only reinforce existing social norms or undertake to improve them. In actuality, our study was undertaken only to determine what, if anything, happens to students, but we have found this a difficult position to sustain and interpret. Any approach to values generates emotional and irrational reactions, both from some of those studied and from some who learn of the findings.

CHANGES IN ATTITUDES, VALUES, AND CRITICAL THINKING

When changes in attitudes, values, and in critical thinking abilities are reported for a group of students, it should be understood what such a reported change means and does not mean. To state, for example, that students became "more liberal" from the freshman to the senior year does *not* mean that *all* students became more liberal. What is meant is that, on the average, the percentage of a group of students responding to one or more statements in a manner somewhat arbitrarily designated as liberal or conservative was greater for these students as seniors than it was as freshmen. Some students may have become more conservative; others may not have changed; but more students accepted the liberal view at the second than at the first response. Despite the *increase* in liberal point of view, the majority response to a statement may still be in the conservative direction. Some few students may have moved from a consistently conservative view on many matters to a consistently liberal one; others may have shifted on only a few items.

In brief, the statement of a statistically significant change in a certain direction must be taken as only an indication that changes were observed, and that they tend, on the average, to be in the stated direction. The change, even though statistically significant, may not be sufficiently great in any one individual that it would be apparent to a friend or interviewer. Furthermore, it is difficult to say whether change in attitudes or values in a given direction is desirable or undesirable. An extremist or dogmatic liberal on a given issue may well become somewhat more conservative, while the extreme conservative becomes more liberal on the same issue. The composite result of such contrasting changes may be equally viewed as an undesirable conformity or as general acceptance of a very moderate position, conducive to constructive compromise. Whereas *improvement* in critical thinking can be accepted as the desirable and unambiguous direction of change, the same cannot be said of changes in attitudes and values. Accordingly, the following statements of results must be viewed as that, and as nothing more than that. Judgments as to desirability or undesirability of the results must be left to those more dogmatic than ourselves.

MAJOR FINDINGS

Since certain terms occur repeatedly in these statements of findings, the following brief definitions will be helpful:

Stereotypic—The stereotypic personality accepts pseudo-rational clichés, is rigid in attitudes and values, and is compulsive and authoritarian in relationship with others.
Dogmatic—The dogmatic personality has fixed views and is unreceptive to new ideas.
Traditional values—Traditional values include belief in personal responsibility, Puritan morality, the work-success ethic, and future-time orientation in contrast to the "emergent" values of sociability, security, group-determined moral standards, and present-time orientation.

BIOGRAPHICAL AND DEMOGRAPHIC DIFFERENCES

(1) Male undergraduates were significantly more stereotypic, dogmatic, and unreceptive to new ideas than females. Males also were significantly more traditional-value-oriented than females.

(2) Catholic students were the most stereotypic and dog-

matic and had the highest traditional-value scores. Jewish students were the least traditional-value-oriented.

(3) There were significant differences in attitudes and values of Protestant students coming from liberal and from fundamentalist sects. The latter were significantly more stereotypic and dogmatic.

(4) There was no significant difference in attitudes and values between those students whose parents were native-born Americans and those students whose parents were foreign-born.

(5) Students from the rural areas had higher mean traditional-value scores than those from urban areas.

(6) Students from the lower socio-economic levels tended to be more stereotypic and have higher traditional-value scores than students from the upper-middle or upper social levels.

(7) Females majoring in the nontechnical curricula were less stereotypic and dogmatic than those in vocationally-oriented programs. Males in the physical and biological sciences were less stereotypic in their beliefs than males enrolled in other fields.

CHANGES FROM FRESHMAN TO SENIOR YEAR

(1) In nearly all instances there appeared a significant improvement in critical thinking ability, a lessening of stereotypic beliefs, and a movement away from the traditional-value-orientation in each of the freshman, sophomore, junior, and senior years. The only exception was for changes in value orientation for both males and females during the senior year. Although the previous college years demonstrated a trend from "inner" to "outer-or-other" directedness, the senior year did not evidence such a change. In fact, it would appear that, after the junior year, a plateau is reached with respect to value orientation of college students.

(2) Students in general became more flexible and less authoritarian from their freshman to senior year; more receptive of people of different races, creeds, and religions; more liberal in their views and opinions about standards of behavior; more aware of their own goals in life; more confident of their ability to deal with new problems; more realistic in outlook toward the

future; and more likely to question the absolutes in life insofar as they pertain to moral and religious conduct.

(3) Although the changes were found each year from the freshman to the senior year, the major changes took place during the first two years of college. In fact, changes in critical thinking ability and in value orientation were of greatest magnitude in the freshman year.

(4) With only one exception (dogmatism for males), there was greater homogeneity at the end of the senior year than there was at the beginning of the freshman year.

(5) Although college freshmen were concerned with obtaining good grades, as seniors they attached even more importance to grades.

(6) College freshmen were concerned with preparation for a specific vocation, but as seniors they attached increased significance to a well-rounded education.

(7) Seniors, to a greater extent than freshmen, felt that college professors should be allowed to subscribe to any political or ideological belief they wish. However, these same students felt that the faculty should not interfere with the students' behavior or beliefs.

(8) A sizable percentage of students indicated that they felt they had undergone no marked change in their attitudes, values, beliefs, and interests while at college.

(9) A small percentage of students changed in what might be termed a negative direction; that is, they became more stereotypic and prejudiced in their views, became less tolerant of others, became less receptive to new ideas, and became more authoritarian.

(10) Although many students felt that during their college careers they became less attached rather than more attached to a particular religious orientation, they reported no diminution of belief in the value of religion in a mature life.

(11) For the males, those who enrolled at Michigan State and attended for four years became less traditional-value-oriented than their counterparts who enrolled at the same time but withdrew from college during their freshman, sophomore, or junior year. In fact, for the male withdrawals, those males who

attended college for 0–3 terms became more traditional-value-oriented (between 1958 and 1962) than their withdrawal counterparts who attended for 4–6 or 7–10 terms. A somewhat similar trend was evident for the change in value orientation for females.

(12) For both males and females, there was no significant relationship between length of college attendance and changes in dogmatism, receptivity to new ideas, or an attitude of open-mindedness. All groups moved toward a more open-minded and flexible attitude.

(13) For both males and females, there was a significant decrease in stereotypic beliefs between 1958 and 1962 regardless of amount of education. For the females only, the intensity of the decrease was related to length of college attendance; that is, the longer a girl attended college, the more likely was she to become less stereotypic in her beliefs in comparison to her counterparts who withdrew before graduation.

INTERRELATIONSHIPS OF VARIOUS FACTORS WITH CONTINUING IN COLLEGE

(1) The analysis of data on freshman year withdrawals suggests that collegiate persistence depends primarily upon intellectual ability, but that certain affective factors, such as attitudes, motivation, and interest, have a definite but individually variable influence.

(2) For both males and females, the inclusion of a battery of affective variables contributed very little to the overall prediction of academic success. This was so whether the measure of academic success is in terms of grade-point average or grades in specific general education courses.

(3) Students who were highly stereotypic and dogmatic tended to receive higher grades from their instructors than were apparently warranted by their general academic aptitude.

(4) There was no significant relationship between amount of college education and certainty of plans for the immediate future. Over fifty per cent of the females and over forty-five per cent of the males, regardless of length of college attendance, felt uncertain regarding their future plans.

(5) Over sixty per cent of the males and females in each of

the groups felt that all college students should be required to take a series of general education courses. Although the period of time in college made no difference among the males in their responses to this item, female seniors were somewhat less favorably inclined toward general education courses than were female freshman and sophomore withdrawals.

(6) The majority of those in the study, regardless of sex and amount of college education, felt that a college education should place equal emphasis on both academic and social aspects of development.

(7) No clear-cut pattern was evident in regard to the relationship between the amount of college education and opinions on selected social, economic, and political issues. On some issues, the findings were in the expected direction (more liberal in accord with the general trend), while in others they were contrary to what would be expected.

(8) Regardless of sex and amount of college education, the majority of subjects felt that Red China should not be admitted to the United Nations, that medical care for the aged should be provided by the federal government, that the United States should continue nuclear testing in the atmosphere, that petting and deep kissing are appropriate sex outlets for unmarried college students, and that a person in a skilled trade is worth as much to society as one in a profession.

(9) Anticipated participation in community activities was greater for those completing more years of college.

(10) Although students in general, regardless of sex and amount of college education, changed in their attitudes, values, beliefs, and opinions between 1958 and 1962, the females underwent a more marked change during this period than did the males. Changes were greater for those completing college than for any of the withdrawal groups.

IMPACT OF COLLEGE

(1) Students, in general, felt that the most significant thing that had happened to them or that they learned while at college was to get along with all types of people. Although many do not necessarily agree with the views and opinions of their peers, they

have developed, or at least adopted, a "live and let live" outlook.

(2) College students, regardless of level, were highly resentful of any rules and regulations which they felt interfered with their independence.

(3) The most significant reported experience in the collegiate lives of these students was their association with different personalities in their living units. The analysis of interview and questionnaire data also strongly suggested that discussions and bull sessions were a potent factor in shaping the attitudes and values of these college students.

(4) Before the junior year, courses and instructors were rarely mentioned as having a marked impact upon student attitudes and values. From the junior year on, however, the formal, academic experiences (especially courses and instructors in the student's major) began to assume an increased, although not predominant, importance. One might conclude that, whereas the formal, academic experiences prior to the junior year were subordinate to the informal, nonacademic experiences, the converse was true after the sophomore year.

(5) Courses and instructors in the general education area were frequently characterized by both juniors and seniors as having had a reinforcing rather than a modifying effect on their personality development.

(6) Of all the course or instructional experiences mentioned by juniors and seniors (both males and females) as having had a reinforcing or modifying effect, instructors and courses in the humanities were most frequently chosen.

(7) Both senior students and former students who had withdrawn felt that the academic values should be of utmost importance to both faculty and students. Being original and creative, demonstrating scholarly capacity, and dedicating oneself to one's studies were factors thought to be important by all, regardless of sex and amount of college education.

COMPARISONS OF M.S.U. STUDENTS WITH STUDENTS IN TWO SMALL LIBERAL ARTS COLLEGES

(1) There did not appear to be an atypical or unique personality characteristic or set of characteristics that distinguished

students at the three colleges surveyed. However, the students at the university had higher critical thinking ability scores.

(2.) After controlling for differences in critical thinking ability among students at three Midwestern colleges (two church-affiliated liberal arts colleges and Michigan State University), the results showed no significant difference in dogmatism or in traditional-value-orientation for either males or females. There was, however, a significant difference in stereotypic beliefs among the males at the three colleges, with such beliefs being more common in the liberal arts colleges.

SOME IMPLICATIONS OF THE STUDY

College students do change during the period of college attendance and, generally speaking, the amount and nature of change are related to the period of time spent at college. However, individual students and identifiable subgroups change in varying degrees and even in different directions. In a large university, the great variety of experiences and subcultures means that the experiences of individuals may be very different, either by chance or by choice. Some students apparently seek new experiences which induce changes, while others seek contacts and experiences which reinforce their present views and prejudices. Reactions of students to experiences also vary. Some, disturbed by their experiences, withdraw from them and from the university; others, equally disturbed, find a challenge and seek a new accommodation to a new world; still others, with restricted patterns of experience, withdraw out of sheer boredom.

Affective factors are involved in college success and are changed by college, but the factors themselves are complex and unclear; they are neither unidimensional nor unidirectional in nature and development. Hence, generalizations as specific and as generally applicable as those which can be made about academic aptitude or critical thinking abilities are not possible. Furthermore, changes in attitudes and values are the result of the interaction of so many factors, including maturation, that it is not possible to say with any certainty what experiences, either in general or in specific cases, have been most productive of change.

Although courses and instructors do seem to have some impact on students' attitudes and values—especially in the final two years—students regard peer-group contacts and nonacademic experiences as more important. Although the results may be, in part, an artifact of the instruments and appraisal procedures, it also seems clear that the major impact of the college on critical thinking, attitudes, and values is made within the first years. Students increase in homogeneity over the four years and, at least in part, they do so by accommodating to prevailing mores or by withdrawing entirely. The enrollment disparity between lower and upper divisions, coupled with widely prevalent faculty emphasis on majors and specialization, tends to focus concern on the junior and senior years—a situation defensible only if a very limited purview is taken of the objectives of higher education. The first two years appear, in many ways, to be more critical than the last two.

There is some indication that students characterized by stereotypic beliefs, rigidity, and an authoritarian orientation receive from some instructors better grades than they deserve, while the critically-minded nonauthoritarian may suffer because he makes his own judgments rather than reflects those of the instructor. This tendency is not of catastrophic proportion, but it illustrates the possibility that an institution may harbor practices and personalities which have an impact contradictory to its announced intent. A college which presumes to have a desirable impact on the critical thinking abilities, attitudes, and values of its students may find that its grading practices, regulations, and policy-making procedures have an undesirable impact controverting the changes sought in students.

Change in college students, as in all human beings, is inevitable over a four-year period. However, change in any specific set of attitudes or values is not necessarily to be found in all students, and probably should not be. A college program so structured as to force acceptance of certain attitudes or values molds a student into a pattern instead of permitting him to develop. Such enforced molding, whatever the techniques used, has no place in higher education. Some students may evince deviant and disconcerting attitudes and values, but, unless these are completely disruptive, we must accept them, for such variations provide evidence that education is developmental and that it encourages individuality in attitude and originality in thinking. We noted that many students seemed to resent the implication that college experiences should change their attitudes and values. Although some students saw little change in themselves, others admitted to change while in college, but objected to relating these changes to specific experiences. We interpret this to mean that students, rightfully, will resent the implication that they are being changed in particular ways without their knowledge or consent. On the other hand, students do agree that the college environment should provide opportunity for *examination* of one's attitudes, values, and thought processes. Change may then occur if the individual so wills it.

Higher education involves a continuing search for answers, not the dissemination of answers. Thus the attitudes, values, and methods characteristic of the scholar in his continuing search for more and better answers must be the concern of higher education. These attitudes, values, and methods may be collectively termed "process values," since they are essential in the process of collecting and organizing knowledge and of making judgments about what decisions or courses of action most likely contribute to securing freedom, justice, beauty, or whatever other values an individual desires to promote.

If the student is to examine his values and internalize a set of attitudes, values, and capabilities of judgment, his total college experience must be considered. The scholarly approach of the classroom must be paralleled by a deliberative approach to all other phases of campus activity. The student must have some degree of trust in his mentors, knowing that years of experience have formed the views they espouse, the methods they present, and the values they hold in the decisions required in the planning and operation of the college and, by extension, to the decisions involved in all phases of living. Only then does the student have an interrelated or integrated educational experience in which the significance and necessity of a value is made evident. Such an educational experience is integrative also, for it forces the student to examine his own values in reference to each decision he makes.

The impact of higher education in the area of values, then, should be found in: (a) increased consciousness of one's own values; (b) increased awareness of value differences and conflicts among individuals and groups; (c) re-examination and possibly modification of one's values; and (d) increased ability to make decisions and take actions which witness and reinforce the values in which one believes.

Our study suggested that these changes, at least in some small measure, took place in many of our students. Unfortunately, this study, like others, was designed more to look for specific changes than for a change in value orientation. Thus research to date reveals something of value change, but it tells very little of the effectiveness of colleges in fostering a value orientation and value-based decisions and actions on the part of our students.

NOTES

1. P. E. Jacob, *Changing Values in Colleges* (New York: Harper & Bros., 1957).

2. S. Arsenian, "Changes in Evaluative Attitude," *Journal of Applied Psychology,* August, 1943, 338–49; E. C. Hunter, "Changes in General Attitudes of Women Students During Four Years of College," *Journal of Social Psychology,* November, 1942, 243–57; and S. L. Pressey, "Changes from 1923 to 1943 in the Attitudes of Public School and University Students," *Journal of Psychology,* January, 1946, 173–88.

3. M. B. Freedman, *The Impact of College,* New Dimensions in Higher Education, No. 4, U. S. Office of Education (Washington: Government Printing Office, 1960).

4. H. Webster, M. B. Freedman, and P. Heist, "Personality Changes in College Students," *The American College,* ed. N. S. Sanford (New York: John Wiley & Sons, 1962).

5. E. D. Eddy, Jr., "Changing Values and Attitudes on the Campus," *Long-Range Planning for Education,* ed. A. E. Traxler (Washington: American Council on Education, 1958); and Eddy, *The College Influence on Student Character* (Washington: American Council on Education, 1959).

6. D. R. Brown and D. Bystrym, "College Environment, Person-

ality, and Social Ideology of Three Ethnic Groups," *Journal of Social Psychology*, November, 1956, 279–88.

7. Eddy, *College Influence*, pp. 9 ff.

8. L. B. Mayhew, "And in Attitudes," *Evaluation in the Basic College*, ed. P. L. Dressel (New York: Harper & Bros., 1958); Jacob, *Changing Values;* and M. Wagman, "Attitude Change and Authoritarian Personality," *Journal of Psychology*, July, 1955, 3–24.

9. P. W. Kurtz, "Human Nature, Homeostasis, and Value," *Philosophy and Phenomenological Research*, September, 1956, 36–55; and C. Morris, *Varieties of Human Value* (Chicago: University of Chicago Press, 1958).

10. L. E. Dameron, "Mother-Child Interaction in the Development of Self-Restraint," *Journal of Genetic Psychology*, June, 1955, 289–308; and J. Hemming, "Some Aspects of Moral Development in a Changing Society," *British Journal of Educational Psychology*, June, 1957, 77–78.

11. H. P. Smith, "Do Intercultural Experiences Affect Attitudes?" *Journal of Abnormal and Social Psychology*, November, 1955, 469–77.

12. H. E. O. James, "Personal Contact in School and Change in Intergroup Attitudes," *International Social Science Bulletin*, January, 1955, 55–60; and F. J. McGuigan, "Psychological Changes Related to Intercultural Experiences," *Psychological Reports*, March, 1958, 55–60.

13. E. N. P. Nelson, "Patterns of Religious Attitude Shift from College to Fourteen Years Later," *Psychological Monographs*, No. 424 (Washington: American Psychological Association, 1956).

14. M. Rosenberg, "Psychological Depression and Educational Attitudes," *Student Medicine*, January, 1956, 5–20.

15. E. R. Carlson, "Attitude Change Through Modification of Attitude Structure," *Journal of Abnormal and Social Psychology*, March, 1956, 256–61; and D. Katz, C. McClintoc, and I. Sarnoff, "The Measurement of Ego-Defense as Related to Attitude Change," *Journal of Personality*, June, 1957, 465–74.

16. Jacob, *Changing Values*.

17. E. Raushenbush, "Changing Values and Attitudes on the Campus—A Look to the Future," *Long-Range Planning for Education*, ed. Traxler.

18. W. T. Plant, *Personality Changes Associated with a College Education* (San Jose, Calif.: San Jose State College, 1962).

10

THE CRITERION PROBLEM IN HIGHER EDUCATION

Donald P. Hoyt*

Donald P. Hoyt, formerly Director of the Counseling Center and Associate Professor of Psychology at Kansas State College, is currently Coordinator of Research Services of the American College Testing Program in Iowa City.

INTRODUCTION

One has only to examine a broad range of typical practices in higher education to arrive at the conclusion that the college grade-point average is employed as a pervasive measure of "general worth." This simple index is used to determine whether or not the student may graduate; whether he should be dismissed or placed on probation; whether he can be admitted to a graduate or professional school; whether he is permitted to enroll in an honors program, independent study, or some other "special" experience; whether he is eligible for a loan or scholarship; and whether he obtains a favorable or unfavorable employment reference. I propose to examine the question, "Do college grades deserve this emphasis?" To do so I shall review relevant literature concerning the predictive meaning of the GPA.

Academicians are generally pleased to cite publications by Bridgman [1] or Walters and Bray [2] which show positive relationships between college standing and salary at A.T. & T. They are less enthralled when the critic shows that the relationships were really quite modest (contingency coefficients of only .37 and

* The assistance of Larry Braskamp is gratefully acknowledged.

.33) or when the suggestion is made that personnel practices at A.T. & T. may have virtually assured a positive, but spurious, relationship. There is pride in Knapp's 1916 report which showed that 41 per cent of Harvard's *summa cum laude* graduates were listed in *Who's Who*,[3] but uneasiness in Olson's recent report that the typical *Who's Who* college graduate was a C+ or B− student.[4] The enthusiasm occasioned by Pierson's 1947 finding that undergraduate GPA in engineering correlated .43 with ratings of success as an engineer[5] is dampened by the observation that success was rated by the same professors who gave the grades. And Beatty and Cleeton's 1928 study of Carnegie Tech graduates[6] or Jepsen's 1951 follow-up of Fresno State graduates[7] both of which found no relationship between grades and salary, are either ignored or used to show that salary really isn't important after all.

GROUND RULES FOR EVALUATING RESEARCH

Perhaps studies like these inspired the famous quotation that statistics are one of the three types of lies. At any rate, it is clear that some ground rules should be established for identifying research which will yield dependable evidence. In a difficult area like this, it is unlikely that *the definitive* study can ever be done. Yet some studies do appear to be more unambiguous than others. The following ground rules help identify such studies:

(1) The samples should be representative of some defined population of college graduates. It should not consist of a select segment of that population, such as Phi Beta Kappas.

(2) Field of endeavor should be controlled. It seems unlikely that any measures of success can be found which will be equally applicable to businessmen, educators, physicians, and research workers.

(3) Differences among colleges should be taken into account. Since colleges are known to attract students with different potentials and to follow somewhat different grading standards, any cross-college studies should adjust for these differences.

(4) The complexity of the criterion problem (what is success?) must be adequately recognized and dealt with. Unless we have confidence that our measures of adult accomplishment are

meaningful, there is little sense in determining whether college grades are related to them.

AN ABBREVIATED LITERATURE REVIEW

By employing these guidelines, it is possible to identify, from approximately fifty studies which have been reported, a handful distinguished by their relative freedom from experimental error. Let me briefly review them:

Business. In the business area, Pallett's recent study of University of Iowa graduates is the most dependable. He dealt with 230 graduates employed in nontechnical aspects of business from five to ten years after college graduation. Using carefully constructed behavioral rating scales, he obtained the appraisals of immediate supervisors with respect to 23 specific dimensions of occupational performance. His "overall success" criterion, a combination of "Progress" and "Potential" ratings, was adequately accounted for by only eight dimensions. Pallett called these eight "elements of success" in general business. College grades were found to be independent of all eight measures; the exact correlations varied from −.05 to +.04.[8]

Medicine. A research team at Utah has completed a significant series of studies on urban and rural general practitioners, college of medicine faculty members, and board-qualified specialists.[9] Through structured interviews, directories and compendiums, faculty and alumni records, curriculum vitae and bibliographies, polled opinions of medical students, medical school departmental chairmen and peers, questionnaires, and official college transcripts, over 200 different measures of performance were collected for each physician. The 80 measures judged most relevant for each of the four subsamples were subjected to factor analysis. These measures included undergraduate GPA, GPA in the first two years of medical school, and GPA during the last two years of medical school for all four groups.

Perhaps the most prominent finding was the complexity of physician performance. From 25 to 29 independent factors were extracted in each of the four samples. While some of the same factors were identified in all samples, a number of factors were found which were unique to a given type of medical practice. Of most importance to the present review was the emergence of academic achievement as a unique factor in each group; that is, academic performance was unrelated to any other dimension of physician performance. Perhaps the most impressive demonstration of this finding came from correlating each of the three measures of academic performance with the other performance measures obtained in each of the four samples. Only three per cent of the 849 correlations were significant; five per cent would be expected by chance. Of those that were significant, there were more negative than positive coefficients.

Scientific Research. A postwar study by the National Advisory Committee on Aeronautics (NACA) showed that quality of research performance was unrelated to college grades.[10] The results were especially surprising since NACA had been forced by the competitive employment situation to hire some college graduates with very poor academic records; thus a limited range in college achievement did not account for these negative results. This study stimulated Taylor, Smith, Ghiselin, and Ellison to undertake a more extensive investigation of the research contributions of 107 physical scientists at two Air Force research centers. An elaborate factor analysis of criterion data produced 14 measurable dimensions of research performance. Only three of these were significantly related to college grades—productivity in written work (r = .27), creativity rating by laboratory chiefs (r = .21), and organizational status (salary, number of supervisees; r = .19). Among the criteria independent of GPA were quality of research work, originality of research work, scientific reputation, and overall performance.[11]

Teaching. Although more studies relating grades to occupational success were found in the teaching area than in any other, none has dealt intensively with the criterion problem. Erickson's 1954 study is one of the most satisfactory. He obtained nine different criterion measures which included ratings by supervisors, outside experts, peers, and pupils. Grade averages in ten different combinations of college courses were used as predictors. None correlated significantly with single criteria. When the ratings were factor-analyzed, practice teaching grade did bear a modest relationship (.28) to two of the factors; none of the other 28 correlations was significantly different from zero.[12]

Non-Vocational Accomplishments. Only two studies were found relating college grades to achievements outside the vocational realm. The widely quoted Plasse study of over 9,000 representative college graduates found correlations ranging from .01 to .07 between college grades and civic participation, social participation, knowledge of current events, and satisfactoriness of home life.[13] Mann's study of Wisconsin graduates produced similarly disquieting results: college grades were unrelated to her measures of cultural interests, citizenship activities, or social status of the home.[14]

INTERPRETATION AND IMPLICATIONS

Despite limitations in these studies, it seems safe to conclude that college grades have no more than a very modest correlation with adult success, no matter how defined. Refinements in experimental methodology are extremely unlikely to alter that generalization; at best they may determine some of the conditions under which a low positive, rather than a zero, correlation is obtained.

Three major implications can be suggested. First, the meaning of grades needs to be empirically determined. Second, evaluation procedures in higher education need to be drastically altered. Third, these changes need to be reflected in policies of selection or acceptance for professional training.

(1) The Meaning of College Grades. Can we conclude from this review that college grades are actually or nearly worthless? No. To do so would necessitate showing that grades are invalid representations of the type of student development which they are designed to reflect.

Traditionally, higher education is said to have three major purposes: to preserve, to pass on, and to enrich the cultural heritage. For the undergraduate student, education focuses almost exclusively on transmitting the cultural heritage. The preservation and enrichment of this heritage is left primarily to scholars and scientists, and to formal preservation devices (such as libraries, museums, galleries, and the professionals who manage them). Undergraduate grades are frequently taken, then, as a relative measure of the degree to which the cultural heritage has been successfully transmitted. In layman's terminology, they presumably tell how much the student knows.

Since there is no necessary relationship between what a person knows and what he does with his knowledge, the validity of grades should be established by determining how well they measure the amount of knowledge the student possesses, not by how "successful" the student is in his subsequent enterprises. Used for such measurement, grades may be valid indices of a student's knowledge. Their failure to predict criteria like those reviewed in this paper hardly constitutes a decisive indictment.

Proponents of this view commonly assert that the traditional measures of adult accomplishment or "success" are highly suspect criteria. Such measures often represent direct or indirect endorsements of a materialistic philosophy which bears little resemblance to higher education's devotion to truth and wisdom. Results reviewed in this paper may even have been "expected," since "success" in today's world is popularly believed to be a more frequent result of the "glad hand" and the "fast shuffle" than the "reasoned plan" and the "informed viewpoint."

Such logic is sufficiently compelling to warn us against the conclusion that grades are worthless. On the other hand, we need not infer that present methods of assigning grades are inherently valid. Data from the American College Testing Program's Research Service consistently show marked inconsistencies in grading standards among colleges, among departments within a college, and among instructors within a department. In view of these findings and the widespread criticism that grades are simply measures of general intelligence, that they reflect only superficial knowledge, that "testwiseness" and sensitivity to instructor biases are significant sources of error, and that the "knowledge" measured is largely transient, it is reasonable to recommend that intensive studies be made to validate how effectively grades measure the transmission of the cultural heritage. In the design of such studies, criterion measures should reflect knowledge of a relatively *permanent* nature and extraneous variables should be carefully controlled.

(2) *Evaluation in Higher Education.* Educational philosophy differs from institution to institution in accordance with differences in charters, facilities, boards, students, and staffs. While most colleges would probably endorse the general purposes just reviewed, many would add other purposes. College catalogs frequently contain statements which imply additional objectives. For example, most colleges profess to perform a "guidance" function, helping the individual identify his strengths and weaknesses and plan his future accordingly. The development of vocational competencies and of general skills (e.g., interpersonal competency, communication skills) are at least implied purposes at most colleges. Attitudinal and value development are likewise common goals (e.g., to increase "tolerance," "objectivity," "esthetic appreciation," etc.). Yet the GPA is the only assessment which is typically made of educational progress, with the exception of the negative assessment assigned the student who violates moral, ethical, or legal standards.

There is good reason for believing that academic achievement (knowledge) and other types of student growth and development are relatively independent of each other.[15] In view of this likelihood and the multiple purposes which characterize goals of higher education, how can educational progress best be assessed? Two alternatives suggest themselves: (1) encourage instructors to grade on the basis of multiple considerations, not knowledge alone; (2) encourage assessment of various characteristics and the subsequent substitution of a "profile of student growth and development" for the present transcript of grades. The second is more appealing than the first. If knowledge is relatively independent of other types of educational growth, a measure which combined multiple indices would be undesirably ambiguous.

On the other hand, the development of a profile would, one hopes, result in broader conceptions of "standards." It should help educators recognize the individual differences which characterize college students and make explicit some of the drawbacks to the "Procrustean bed" approach to education. College students have different potentials and different temperaments; "development" can most meaningfully be conceptualized, then, from the individual's frame of reference. The plea is not to lower standards but to individualize them more; to encourage and stimulate personal development in whatever dimensions it is best expressed. To be concrete, it means we would be willing to "forgive" a student his inability (or unwillingness) to master a foreign language if he manifested alternative signs of personal development (e.g., composed publishable music, developed his potential for leadership). Dramatic changes in both evaluation and programming in higher education would be the inevitable result of broadening our conception of educational development.

How could such a profile be developed? What new measuring devices would be needed? It would be presumptuous to attempt a complete answer to these questions. Two suggestions can be offered, however.

First, it seems unlikely that the beleaguered instructor can provide a very comprehensive assessment. His opportunity to observe is limited both by the artificial classroom setting and by the necessity of his concentrating his energy on instruction rather than appraisal. The exhaustive work of Davis at the Educational Testing Service is relevant. He found that, while faculty members used sixteen different dimensions in describing desirable student characteristics, only three were unsatisfactorily reflected by grades. These were "ethicality," "likeableness," and "altruism." [16] There may be some value in seeking faculty ratings on such characteristics, but the faculty's focus on intellectual attainment is likely to interfere with their ability to appraise other types of development.

Second, research at the ACT program [17] and elsewhere has made it clear that checklists of accomplishments can be relatively easily developed to summarize significant indications of personal and professional development. Students can do, and do do, a number of things to demonstrate their potentials. A continuous and systematic accounting of such student behaviors as completing a committee assignment, discussing a matter in depth with a professor, adapting a piece of existing equipment to a new problem, organizing a drive for votes or funds, or establishing a small business, would produce a considerably richer picture of student growth and development than the transcript of grades can ever provide.

The preceding discussion admittedly goes beyond the data now at hand. Its key assumption, that college grades measure only one relatively independent aspect of educational development, has not been thoroughly established. But it seems demonstrably more consistent with reason and research than the alternative supposition that grades are valid measures of "general worth."

(3) *Selection of Students for Professional Training.* There is another, perhaps less controversial, problem in higher education for which the present review has implications: namely, admission of students to upper division or professional departments. The practice of basing admission to schools of education, business, engineering, or medicine largely or exclusively on undergraduate grades seems indefensible. It is certain that many potential contributors in these fields are denied the opportunity for professional training. These personal tragedies must represent a sizeable loss to society as well.

Curricula for which professional preparation is a primary goal should accept those students whose potential is greatest for making a professional contribution. Clearly, a more comprehensive assessment of student characteristics than the transcript of grades can provide will be needed. The present review gives little support to the practice of establishing a relatively high "cut-off" in terms of GPA and then considering "other characteristics" in selecting a professional class.

A professional department bears an inescapable obligation to evaluate the professional promise and preparation of the student. Society must be protected from the incompetent, and the employers of college graduates have a right to know their strengths and weaknesses. College grades fall far short as comprehensive measures of professional promise or competency.

It is hard to be optimistic that selection and evaluation procedures can be effectively changed immediately. The same complexities which plagued the research reviewed in this paper guarantee no easy solutions. Improved procedures depend upon research which relates personal characteristics to performance measures. But if we hope to advance tomorrow, we must begin this frustrating and exciting work today.

SUMMARY

Research findings have consistently shown that college grades have no practical value in forecasting the level of post-college achievement. This embarrassing generalization should stimulate us to examine our methods of appraising educational progress. There is good reason to suggest that, even if present methods of assigning grades have validity, the picture of student development provided by the academic transcript is extremely narrow. A more comprehensive assessment of a variety of achievement dimensions is needed. Such an assessment should stimulate new programs designed to promote a broad range of student competencies and potentials; it should also lead to more realistic, fairer processes for selecting students for professional and graduate schools. The problem requires creative research, imaginative educational programming, and courageous administrative decisions.

NOTES

1. D. S. Bridgman, "Success in College and Business," *Personnel Journal,* Vol. 9 (1930), 1–19.

2. R. W. Walters and D. W. Bray, "Today's Search for Tomorrow's Leaders," *Journal of College Placement,* Vol. 24 (1963), 22–23.

3. R. M. Knapp, "The Man Who Led His Class in College—and Others," *Harvard Graduate Magazine,* Vol. 24 (1916), 597–600.

4. M. S. Olson, "Majority in *Who's Who* Not Top Students," cited in J. H. Sanberg, "Little Case Studies for a Modern Course in Classroom Management," *Phi Delta Kappan,* Vol. 46 (1965), 441.

5. G. A. Pierson, "School Marks and Success in Engineering," *Educational Psychological Measurement,* Vol. 7 (1947), 612–17.

6. J. D. Beatty and G. U. Cleeton, "Predicting Achievement in College and After Graduation," *Personnel Journal,* Vol. 6 (1928), 344–51.

7. V. L. Jepsen, "Scholastic Proficiency and Vocational Success,"

Educational Psychological Measurement, Vol. 11 (1951), 616–28.

8. J. E. Pallett, "Definition and Prediction of Success in the Business World" (unpublished Ph.D. dissertation, University of Iowa, Iowa City, 1965).

9. P. B. Price, *et al.,* "Measurement of Physician Performance," *Journal of Medical Education,* Vol. 39 (1964), 203–211; J. M. Richards, Jr., *et al.,* "An Investigation of the Criterion Problem for One Group of Medical Specialists," *Journal of Applied Psychology,* Vol. 49 (1965), 79–90; C. W. Taylor, *et. al.,* "An Investigation of the Criterion Problem for a Medical School Faculty," *Journal of Applied Psychology,* Vol. 48 (1964), 294–301; and Taylor, *et al.,* "A Study of the Criterion Problem for a Group of Medical General Practitioners," *Journal of Applied Psychology,* Vol. 49, No. 6 (1965), 399–406.

10. Reported in C. W. Taylor, W. R. Smith, and B. Ghiselin, "The Creative and Other Contributions of One Sample of Research Scientists," *Scientific Creativity: Its Recognition and Development,* ed. Taylor and F. Barron (New York: John Wiley & Sons, 1963).

11. C. W. Taylor, *et al., Explorations in the Measurement and Prediction of Contributions of One Sample of Scientists,* Report ASD-TR 61–96, Aeronautical Systems Division, Personnel Laboratory (Lackland Air Force Base, Texas: 1961).

12. H. E. Erickson, "A Factorial Study of Teaching Ability," *Journal of Experimental Education,* Vol. 23 (1954), 1–39.

13. W. Plasse, "Comparison of Factors in Achievement in College and Adult Life" (unpublished Ph.D. dissertation, Syracuse University, Syracuse, N. Y., 1951).

14. Sister M. Jacinta Mann, "Relationship Among Certain Variables Associated with College and Post-College Success" (unpublished Ph.D. dissertation, University of Wisconsin, Madison, 1958).

15. J. L. Holland and J. M. Richards, Jr., "Academic and Non-Academic Accomplishment: Correlated or Uncorrelated?" in *Journal of Educational Psychology,* Vol. 56 (1965), 165–74.

16. J. A. Davis, *Faculty Perceptions of Students, IV: Desirability and Perception of Academic Performance,* Research Bulletin RB-64–13 (Princeton, N. J.: Educational Testing Service, 1964).

17. C. Abe, *et al., A Description of American College Freshmen,* ACT Research Report, No. 1 (1965), p. 65.

11

THE CONTRIBUTIONS AND IMPLICATIONS OF RECENT RESEARCH RELATED TO IMPROVING TEACHING AND LEARNING

Laurence Siegel

Laurence Siegel began large-scale research endeavors in higher education at Miami University (Ohio) in 1956. He has published widely in journals and edited *Instruction: Some Contemporary Viewpoints*. In September, 1966, he became Chairman of the Department of Psychology at Louisiana State University.

I have recently completed two experiences from which I will draw for this essay: editing *Instruction: Some Contemporary Viewpoints,*[1] and completing and now writing a report of the results (with Lila Corkland Siegel) of a four-year research project on the "Instructional Gestalt." *

The first of these experiences enables me to draw upon both the research and the thinking about research of the following colleagues: James Hedegard, Carl Rogers, Asahel Woodruff, Bruce Biddle, Stanford Ericksen, John Jahnke, David Ausubel, and Robert Gagné. The second represents a deep personal investment of time and energy and undoubtedly colors virtually everything I will have to say. Both experiences are extremely rich

---

* Under grant to Miami University from the Office of Education, United States Department of Health, Education, and Welfare. (Reported as *The Instructional Gestalt in Televised University Courses,* June, 1966, Bureau of Research No. 5–0852.)

mines from which I will be able only to skim what I consider to be the most fertile ore.

In this essay I shall not present data from specific investigations. Instead, I shall discuss what I see as threads common to big chunks of research on classroom teaching and learning; I will react to these in an entirely personal manner by stating my perceptions of their implications for the conduct of higher education in the future.

THE INSTRUCTIONAL GESTALT AS A CONCEPTUAL VIEWPOINT

To begin, it often helps the reader to know something about the source of a writer's biases and orientation. When I joined the staff of Miami University, my purpose was to design and execute a series of evaluative studies to answer the general question: "Is large group instruction (lecture, televised, etc.) as effective and efficient as small group 'conventional' instruction?" This was over ten years ago; and although large classes were by no means a novelty, the question was a revolutionary one for Miami University and other similar institutions. At the inception of the study, we had only one room that could accommodate more than forty students, and that was an auditorium with *very* squeaky chairs. Four years and a quarter of a million dollars later, we were able to say that students appeared to learn as much—or as little—regardless of *how* they were taught.

This type of comparison between instructional procedures, usually television vs. "conventional" instruction, was repeated on several other campuses by other investigators, with essentially similar findings. Furthermore, there have been parallel comparisons involving manipulations of such conditions as class size, number of class meetings, teaching technique, etc.; all of these investigations have resulted in an essentially similar conclusion.

While we concede this, we all know it to be wrong. Our own experiences both as students and teachers reassure us that, data to the contrary, it *does* make a difference how we teach and are taught. Many of us recall a teacher who affected our destiny, a course that helped shape our future, an experience in class that either lit a fire or put one out. Why, then, should the type of comparisons described in the preceding paragraphs produce findings of "no significant differences" with such monotonous regularity?

SOME DIFFICULTIES WITH INSTRUCTIONAL COMPARISONS

One reason is that our criterion measures generally are extremely crude. The final examination, or its derivative, the course grade, has such an honored place in the protoplasm of the university that it was often pressed into service as a research criterion for assessing instructional outcomes. Unfortunately, since course examinations written by teachers tend too much to sample rote factual recall, these examination scores correlate most highly with tests of memory or of general academic ability and with other course grades. It is patently absurd to expect these criteria to reflect modifications in instructional procedure. And even if they *had* been sensitive to such modifications, the value of the findings would be doubtful.

In this regard it is important to note that when an occasional statistically significant difference was reported for instructional procedure comparisons, the criterion had been a function designated "critical thinking" or "problem solving" or "synthesis." The fact that significant differences with these criteria were not obtained more frequently is mute testimony to the relative lack of concern, until recently, with ways in which college teachers could encourage this kind of behavior.

A second reason for the ever-present finding of "no significant difference" is that the comparative procedure itself masked important differences. The mean performance scores that were compared were comprised of individual students' scores both below and above the means. Given any kind of instruction, some students will do relatively well, and others will do rather poorly. The mean obliterates this important piece of information. When two means (derived from two procedures) are compared, we find out only how *groups* fared under these procedures: we lose the important interaction between student and procedure. The usual statistics of control-group comparisons obscure the fact that whereas Procedure I, let's say, is better for Student A than B, Procedure II is better for Student B than A.

In passing, I wish only to mention a third source of difficulty with many of the instructional comparisons reported in the literature—the instructional procedures constituting the experimental conditions tend to be too grossly defined. What do we mean, for example, by lecture instruction, discussion instruction, televised instruction, or conventional instruction? There are literally as many varieties of each of these as there are teachers to provide them and combinations of students to fill the classes.

A DIFFERENT PARADIGM FOR RESEARCH

It was from considerations like those stated above that we decided to use an entirely different strategy in attempting to understand what goes on in a college classroom. The paradigm we sought would enable us to investigate the unique mix of instructor behavior, environmental circumstances, and learner characteristics that comprised a particular instructional setting. We were specifically interested in the *interaction* between learner characteristics (e.g., motivation, academic ability, educational set), instructor action (e.g., the kinds of examinations administered, the type if any of personal contact with students), and features of the learning environment (e.g., amount and type of supervision). This mix is what we have termed the "instructional Gestalt."

Temporarily ignoring our findings, let us consider the implication of this paradigm for research. Instead of thinking in terms of a *best* way to teach something, it assumes—or at least makes it possible to demonstrate—that there are *optimal* ways to teach something to particular students. What "works" for one student need not work for another. The burden of the investigations that follow this paradigm is to discover what works for whom and why.

The learner assumes his proper place in the center of the educational research stage. But since there are many different kinds of learners and many different kinds of instructional objectives, any course is really a series of plays running concurrently—in spite of the fact that they are all simultaneously running in the same theatre. This paradigm was developed to help us discover why some of these are "hits" and others "flops." Its payoff will come when we can identify these principles that will enable us to maximize the attainment of particular *objectives* by each of the students and to translate these principles into action, i.e., into instructional *processes* appropriate to particular instructional *participants*.

The following sections consider these three concepts— objectives, processes, and participants—as organizers for summarizing and integrating substantial blocks of recent (and some not-so-recent) research and thinking about instruction.

INSTRUCTIONAL OBJECTIVES

Teachers, administrators, students, and researchers do not all necessarily agree on the purposes of instruction—objectives are viewed from different positions. At the risk of considerable oversimplification, one might suggest that teachers seek to communicate something about a discipline in which they have a heavy stake; administrators want the university to communicate something about the segment of society in which *it* has a heavy stake; students want whatever is communicated to them to be personally relevant and "real"; and researchers would like the instructional objectives, whatever their nature, to be defined with sufficient precision to permit evaluation.

Taking a less egocentric view, one may find that education has historically been concerned with three fundamental objectives: moral development, adaptability, and ego-development. The first of these, moral development, is implicit in classroom activities; but, with the exception of religious education, it has received little systematic consideration. This is somewhat surprising because teachers and administrators alike seem committed to developing ethical-social morality. The school is a partner in this endeavor, supplementing the efforts of other social institutions. Recognition of the school's role in this partnership is evident from the scrutiny given by Boards of Trustees to library holdings, assigned readings, and teachers' activities both in and out of class. The tradition of academic freedom is tempered by society's investment in perpetuating the values it presently holds. To a large extent, universities tend to mirror rather than shape societal views of social-political issues. Instructional researchers generally avoid this issue.

In contrast, all parties to instruction either imply or state outright the value they put upon adaptive behavior rather than the acquisition of knowledge and skill. We all emphasize creativity, synthesis, conceptualization, problem solving, and thinking—at least in our words if not in our deeds. We regard facts merely as intellectual tools.

Ego-development also is generally accepted as an instructional objective. Formal education should make a difference to the student not only while he is in school, but also after he has been graduated. Carl Rogers is especially articulate in arguing for educational experiences that have an organismic impact upon the learner. He writes that such experiences must have the qualities of personal involvement, self-initiated learning, pervasiveness, a locus of evaluation internal to the learner, and personal meaning and relevance to the learner.[2]

If we can agree on adaptability and ego-development as the most important educational objectives, then we can agree on the fundamental purpose of instruction: to structure the conditions of education so as to permit students to attain these objectives. The attainment of this purpose in a classroom involves two essential processes—learning and teaching—and two essential participants—students and teachers or teacher-substitutes.*

PROCESSES AND PARTICIPANTS

Learning and Learners. The investigator's question when he studies the learning process is simple enough: "How do students come to modify their beliefs and their behavior?" Once phrased, this question must inevitably be elaborated by specifying *what* is to be learned, although the language of elaboration differs among educational objectives and the processes appropriate for their attainment. In its most simple form, this distinction dif-

---

* I have deliberately eliminated from this discussion those interpersonal processes occurring between persons other than teachers and learners both in and out of the classroom and affecting instructional outcomes. I have likewise elected not to be concerned here with such ancillary instructional participants as the student's family, teacher's colleagues, student's living group, etc.

ferentiates between factual versus conceptual acquisition; or, if you wish, between rote versus meaningful learning; or, if you prefer, between associational versus experimental learning. On the one hand, the student acquires knowledge by memorizing or imitating; on the other, he generates his knowledge by thinking. There are two striking things about this type of distinction between instructional objectives. First, and most apparent, virtually everyone who writes about higher education treats as primary the "higher order" objectives such as thinking, conceptualizing, synthesizing, and openness to experience. Whereas teachers, administrators, and students who are on the line, so to speak, often verbalize these as their goals, they frequently settle for much less.

Second, and perhaps less apparent, is the artificiality of attempted distinctions between cognitive and non-cognitive processes when these higher order objectives are emphasized. Such learning involves both the intellect and the viscera. The learner's attitudes, drives, and emotions interact with his sensory impressions and intellectual endowment jointly to determine the overall impact of instruction. Learning is a unitary process involving the total organism.

Learning Is Idiosyncratic. Classes do not learn; students learn, and the progress of learning for any student is marked by spurts, regressions, and apparent plateaus. Thus when we speak of the "best" instructional arrangement for a *class,* we are perpetuating a fiction unless students are selectively assigned to *that* class rather than to some other with a different instructional arrangement. A view of instruction based upon our knowledge about learning is that to be efficient, instruction must so arrange the situational variables that they interact optimally with the learner variables.

Learning Is An Active Process. Contemporary society requires active student involvement and participation in learning. If we continue to treat students as passive reactors—as persons to whom something is done—rather than as active participants, they will seek opportunities for participation and involvement outside the classroom.

The activity, participation, and involvement to which I refer is not to be confused with the simple expedient of having students "take part" by doing something. Although a laboratory exercise, for example, requires activity from the student, it may or may not contribute effectively to his learning. The kind of activity I have in mind requires that learners perceive what they are doing as personally relevant. Participation and involvement cannot be inferred from the superficial appearance of the instructional setting. Some students listening to a lecture may be very active participants; others, despite their exposure to what have been termed "discovery experiences," may be passive.

The Movement Away from Classical Learning Theories. The National Society for the Study of Education entitled its 1964 Yearbook *Theories of Learning and Instruction.* In a postscript to the volume, the editor, Ernest Hilgard, notes that the era of the "great debate" among learning theorists is over.[3] I have noted the same phenomenon in editing *Instruction: Some Contemporary Viewpoints.* Instead of searching for generalized theories of learning applicable to instruction, attention is increasingly being given to developing theories of *particular kinds* of learning.

As they pertain to instruction, this means that such clusters of learning theory as "S-R," "cognitive," "identification," and so on are regarded as compatible rather than competitive. Each one is valid for particular kinds of persons learning particular things in particular situations. Since there are several kinds of learning, it is plausible to posit the existence of an equal number of conditions of effective learning, i.e., optimal instructional conditions.

Teaching and Teachers

Following this argument, *effective* teaching is that which arranges instructional conditions in an optimal fashion. The mediator of effective teaching may be either a person (the teacher) or a teacher-substitute (as in the case of programmed instruction). As a matter of fact, virtually all kinds of "instructional materials"—including books, programs, and laboratory exercises, to name a few—are capable of serving as effective teacher-substitutes if the circumstances are right. These materials may encourage learning and, at least under certain conditions, can provide the student with feedback about his performance.

An inherent limitation of instructional materials, however, is that they are relatively inflexible and therefore insensitive to individual differences among learners. The flexibility that can be built in, for example, by arranging branches in programmed instructional materials, is relatively insignificant compared with the potential flexibility of human teachers.

Prescriptions for "how to teach effectively" are about as outdated as leeching. When offered and implemented, they sap the vigor of both students and teachers. In their place, teachers need to know the goals toward which they are striving and the persons they are teaching. With this knowledge, and assuming subject-matter competence, the teacher can do three things: (1) He can organize his teaching content so it encourages learning most effectively; (2) he can manage or structure the learning environment of his class to consist of micro-environments, each of which is appropriate for *some* of his students; (3) he can catalyze learning in which he cannot participate directly because of either personal or situational limitations.

Moreover, one teacher alone within the context of a university cannot function effectively in these ways without the support of the entire institution. Instructional objectives, whatever their nature, must pervade the curriculum before we insist that they become objectives of individual teachers. The learner's life space includes more than his experiences with any one teacher or set of teachers. This is one point at which an office of instructional (as distinguished from institutional) research can make a highly significant contribution to the effectiveness of the university.

Given the pressures for enrollment with consequent increases in class size, and given the psychological naïveté of most teachers—who after all are specialists in some other discipline— teachers cannot really know the persons they are teaching unless they (the teachers) are assisted in this regard. Somehow, information accumulated by undergraduate advisors, residence hall counselors, the university testing service, the admissions office, and the student's previous instructors must be made accessible to the teachers he now has.

TWO ORGANIZING CONCEPTS: INSTRUCTIONAL PRESS AND IDIOSYNCRATIC DRIVE PATTERNS

Our studies of the instructional Gestalt have led us to formulate two organizing concepts to help us understand and explain substantial masses of data on teaching and classroom learning. One of these concepts, that of *instructional press*, leads to predictions about the impact upon students of the particular way in which the instructional environment is managed. The other concept, that of *idiosyncratic drive patterns*, leads to predictions about the role of particular learner characteristics as partial determinants of the power and impact of specific instructional circumstances.

Instructional Press. The press to which I am referring here is restricted to the classroom and results from the way in which the course is conducted. On the basis of our work, we believe we have evidence for three kinds of instructional presses. In some classes student performance seems highly dependent upon the instructor's behavior and the environmental surroundings. We refer to the instructional press in these instances as *extrinsic*. In other classes, perhaps of the same course, student performance appears to reflect characteristics of the learner more than the instructor-environment conditions. Here we speak of the instructional press as being *intrinsic*. In still other classes, where performance reflects both learner characteristics and instructor-environment conditions, we refer to a *mixed* instructional press.

Etiology of Instructional Presses. We believe at this point that the instructor is a key determinant of the press prevailing in his class. He communicates an attitude to his students by such behavior as his enthusiasm for the subject matter, the organization of his lectures, and his rapport with the class. By his actions the instructor implies to his students that he regards them as intellectually mature or immature—i.e., as capable of coping with appropriately difficult subject matter and assuming appropriate responsibility for their own learning, or as requiring an oversimplified presentation and continual supervision in order to learn. An instructor who regards his students as intellectually mature generates an intrinsic instructional press. One who regards his students as intellectually immature generates an extrinsic instructional press.

Effects of Instructional Presses. The significance of instructional press as a concept is, of course, that different presses are presumed to be associated with corresponding differences in the effectiveness of instruction.

Assuming that an intrinsic press results when the instructor behaves as if the students are intellectually mature, then these students ought in turn to emphasize in their perceptions the potentially supportive aspects of the instructional environment. They should see the instructor as helpful rather than punitive, his examinations as fair rather than unjust, and so on. Conversely, if an extrinsic press results when the instructor behaves as if his students are intellectually immature, these students ought to emphasize in their perceptions the potentially punitive or threatening aspects of the instructional environment.

Hence we regard the instructional press of the classroom as a differential power factor affecting educational performance. Whereas all instructional environments are potentially punitive (or threatening) and potentially supportive to some students, the former aspect is seen as more powerful in the context of an extrinsic instructional press and the latter as more powerful in the context of an intrinsic instructional press.

For our first organizing concept we have the following generalization: *An extrinsic instructional press sensitizes students to the potentially punitive and threatening (inhibiting) aspects of the instructional environment. An intrinsic instructional press sensitizes students to the potentially supportive (facilitating) aspects of the instructional environment.*

But for *whom* is an aspect of the environment potentially inhibiting or potentially facilitating? This is the question to which our second organizing concept, that of idiosyncratic drive pattern, is addressed.

Idiosyncratic Drive Patterns. The distinction is often made between students who learn because they "want to learn" and those whose learning is motivated by such external rewards as graduation and earning approbation. Every student is sufficiently complex that both kinds of factors are at least partially responsible for his learning; but in individual instances, one or the other is weighted more heavily. This idiosyncratic drive mix is brought into the classroom and may either be further reinforced by the instructional setting or conflict with the structure and demands of that setting.

The student's idiosyncratic drive patterns probably control his educational performance in at least two ways. First, they determine the appropriateness or inappropriateness *for him* of selected aspects of the instructional setting. Obviously, provision of considerable opportunity for personal contact with the instructor, for example, is most appropriate for students needing a nurturant relationship and least appropriate for students not needing such a relationship. Second, his idiosyncratic drive patterns help shape the student's perceptions about and his approach to the course. We would expect a student taking a course primarily to fulfill a requirement, for example, to respond to it quite differently from one who enrolls because of a genuine pre-professional commitment to the discipline.

Kinds of Idiosyncratic Drive Patterns. Although there are undoubtedly many kinds of idiosyncratic drive patterns, we believe we have identified two that are especially powerful predictors of educational performance. One of these is a function of the student's academic ability; the other is a function of his educational set—his predisposition for learning "factual" or "conceptual" content. We view the origin of both patterns as current end products of the student's past history of successes and failures for cognitive attainments. They are "givens" with which he enters every course.

Etiologies of Idiosyncratic Drive Patterns. In the case of ability-linked drive patterns, it seems self-evident that high- and low-ability college students have experienced quite different educational histories. High-ability students have probably experienced an educational history replete with positive reinforcement. Their attempts to learn prior to coming to college have probably sufficiently succeeded by external standards that they have developed a self-image of "academic capability." Secure in their capacity for learning, they are relatively free to pick and choose what they wish to learn and to determine for themselves the amount of effort they wish to devote to particular kinds of acquisition.

Low-ability students, on the other hand, have more probably experienced a number of educational failures. Certainly their academic experiences have taught them that in order to attain a given level of academic performance they must expend greater effort over a longer time than their brighter associates.

Set-linked drive patterns likewise reflect different pre-college histories. Contrary to what we might expect, the correlation between educational set and academic ability tends to be low (about .25), with a slight tendency for high-ability students to be conceptually set and for low-ability students to be factually set. Many high-ability students, however, are set to learn factual content, and many low-ability students are set to learn conceptual content. Therefore, although we believe that a student's educational set reflects the learning orientation for which he has been most consistently reinforced, we have speculated that this set is established even more by pre-school than by in-school experiences.

Effects of Idiosyncratic Drive Patterns. Without citing the data, I shall simply summarize what we think we have learned about the influence of idiosyncratic drive patterns. Our premise held that these patterns determine whether the instructional environment is perceived by the student as supportive, in which case his performance *may* be facilitated, or as punitive and/or threatening, in which case his performance *may* be inhibited. The reason for saying "may" rather than "will" be facilitated or inhibited is, of course, that the idiosyncratic drive patterns interact with what we have already described as instructional press. A potential facilitator becomes in fact a facilitator when the instructional press is intrinsic. Likewise, a potential inhibitor becomes in fact an inhibitor when the instructional press is extrinsic.

For ability-linked drive, we believe we have demonstrated that performance by low-ability students is facilitated when the instructional environment insulates them from intellectual threat and/or provides them with academic guidance. The converse of these conditions inhibits performance by low-ability students.

High-ability students perform best when the instructional environment offers appropriate intellectual challenges, whereas their performance is inhibited when the environment presents inappropriately easy or unchallenging material.

This means, in effect, that if the instructional press is arranged properly, the performance of low-ability students can be maximized by placing them in educational settings that are "protective," i.e., wherein the instructor cannot probe in an intellectually embarrassing fashion. Specifically, this means that low-ability students will learn most of what they are capable of learning in classes conducted by television, perhaps with substantial segments committed to programmed instruction. High-ability students will learn most of what *they* are capable of learning in classes permitting intense and probing discussions. It must be reëmphasized, however, that these effects can be "washed out" and even reversed by what we have termed an extrinsic instructional press.

For set-linked drive, we believe we have demonstrated that student performance may be adversely affected when their set conflicts with the teacher's instructional emphasis. The student, for example, who enters the course with a set to learn concepts but is compelled by examination pressures to learn many miniscule facts will not learn *either* concepts or facts as well as he might. Consequently, if we are concerned solely with maximizing educational performance, it follows that we must allow students who are set to learn concepts to pursue this direction and allow students who are set to pursue facts to pursue *that* direction.

SOME IMPLICATIONS

The research findings summarized above all point to a single conclusion: to be most effective, instruction must be tailored to the needs, capabilities, and histories of the individual learners. The paradox for higher education in contemporary society is that in spite of enrollment pressures and consequent increases in the number of students that must be assigned to each teacher, the desirability of custom-tailoring instruction to the student confronts us. This dilemma means that changes in some prevalent higher education practices are indicated. It also lends an air of urgency to some presently unresolved questions and issues. We need open-mindedly to re-examine our aims, curricula, and teaching practices.

Aims and Curricula. The search for greater "efficiency" in higher education is too often seduced by the model for increasing the efficiency of industrial organizations. For the latter, raising output while holding or reducing costs is a valid gain. In education, however, even if we can increase output with or without a corresponding increase in expenditures, we must question whether it is worthwhile doing more of whatever it is that we now do. Merely holding the line on quality while increasing quantity is probably not enough since our graduates must be prepared for societal and technological changes the specific nature of which cannot be anticipated with certainty.

Aims. Institutions of higher education must make some decisions about their roles as agents for effecting personal change. Assuming that this is a feasible route toward optimizing educational attainments, I must add something about the attainments that deserve to be optimized.

In view of the range of attainments upon which higher education can focus, it seems to me imperative that priorities be assigned so that the most important ones are emphasized by the *entire curriculum.* Without such priorities, the best we shall be able to do is to identify those needs carried into a classroom by a student and arrange circumstances accordingly to facilitate efficient learning in that course. A *pervasive* institutional philosophy—as distinguished from a handful of committed teachers—is required to prevent wasting student talent. No society—not even an affluent one—should permit a substantial number of potentially capable college students to bloom late, wilt early, or never to bloom at all.

In assigning priorities to the aims of higher education, top billing must be accorded such objectives as "adaptability" and "conceptualization." In probing their implementation, we find that these constructs must be reduced to intensely personal and concrete goals that will suggest appropriately personal and concrete curricula and instructional methods.

Curricula. At least three very specific areas of knowledge, understanding, and appreciation underlie the attainment of these goals: the past, the present, and oneself.

An understanding and appreciation of the past— communicated particularly through history and literature— serves at least two ends. First, it provides vicarious experiences which, in part, compensate for the severe limitations upon direct experience possible within a single lifetime. History and literature telescope experience for us. They enable us to grow without risking injury and to think without having to work out of each deadend encountered by our predecessors. Secondly, these disciplines, along with philosophy, provide perspective. An appreciation and understanding of the continuity between past and present and of man's previous attempts to impose order upon the unknown facilitates "conceptualization."

But knowledge of the past and of the continuity of past, present, and future is not alone enough. People must understand themselves and others if they are to contribute to and function in society most effectively. The need for such understanding is by no means reduced in an era of rapid scientific and technological advancement. Because of their specialized knowledge, scientists must assume far greater rather than lesser social responsibility for the impact of their discoveries and innovations.

Universities and colleges can contribute to the realization of these goals in several ways. First, the curriculum must be freed from the artificial compartmentalization of knowledge as represented by discrete courses and textbooks. We all recognize that each discipline is simply a way of looking at the world, emphasizing some of its attributes and deëmphasizing others. To counteract the inevitable distortions produced by these distinctions of convenience, students must be made to feel the interrelatedness of knowledge.

Second, the behavioral sciences must be made more central to curriculum planning and implementation. By this I mean not only that principles from the behavioral sciences ought to determine the arrangement of the curriculum and instructional experiences but also that psychology, sociology, and anthropology be accorded more central status as components of that curriculum. The world is populated by people; in learning about it and in developing a personal relationship to it, students need to know as much as we can tell them about human behavior. The development of sensitivity, empathy, and self-knowledge is too critical to be left to chance.

Third, teachers themselves must have a better understanding of human behavior than is now usually the case. It seems to me remarkable that we so often entrust such great responsibility for shaping the values and destinies of each coming generation to persons who may lack such understanding, both as regards themselves and the students they instruct.

Articulation of Instruction. In addition to articulation of the university curriculum, more attention needs to be given the matter of articulation of instructional levels. The recurring emphasis upon higher order cognitive attainments, particularly at the college level, implies that before entering college the students have developed a sufficiently broad and integrated cognitive structure, a sense of responsibility for directing their own learning, and a set to synthesize and conceptualize.

The notion of an integrated instructional complex extending from elementary grades through higher education with opportunities for branching on the basis of student need and interest is being implemented to a limited degree. An ambitious experiment in articulated instruction of this sort is being undertaken, for example, at the South Florida Education Center (Fort Lauderdale), consisting of Nova elementary and secondary schools, Broward Junior College, and the projected Nova University of Advanced Technology. As we move closer to the time when fifty per cent of our high school graduates will be pursuing some kind of higher education, it grows increasingly imperative that this type of articulation become the norm rather than the exception.

Curricula and Tradition. Undergraduate curricula have, in some degree, been enslaved by the traditions of which they were born. There are limits to the extent to which we can expect successfully to superimpose elements of an educational "new look" upon the existing structure. As with a building, a foundation will accommodate only so many modifications before it creaks, cracks, and finally collapses. I have elected to raise some questions and suggest some changes in four curricular cornerstones.

One cornerstone of our curricular foundation seriously in need of review is the widespread credit-accumulation plan. In this plan, each three-credit course constitutes approximately $\frac{1}{40}$th of an "education"; students are expected to complete $\frac{1}{8}$th of their "education" thus defined each semester by taking five such courses. This requirement necessarily impedes any serious attempt to implement programs of independent study, for example, by fixing the amount of time and effort a student is expected to devote to such a program and by defining the intellectual boundaries of such study. In effect, he studies independently with a view to satisfying the instructor that he has learned whatever he would have learned if he had elected instead to attend the instructor's course.

Another such cornerstone is the usual system of course examinations and grades. Without the assistance of a university examinations service, the tests most instructors develop are probably not suitable for assessing what the student has acquired from the course. More importantly, the potential diagnostic value of course examinations and their potential value for guiding each student into those educational experiences most likely to be valuable for him subsequently is almost invariably lost.

A third curricular cornerstone is the freshman year. In our attempts to process students, we are forced to increase class sizes in freshman courses particularly and to make graduate students increasingly responsible for freshman instruction. This is a time of trauma for many students. The competition for survival is keen; the community of scholars sometimes resembles a community of gladiators.

In addition to its psychic cost, the freshman year must be reckoned as a serious drain upon the financial resources of publicly assisted four-year institutions. Direct instructional costs for courses taken exclusively or primarily by freshmen account for one-third or more of an institution's total undergraduate instructional budget. Probably only between forty and forty-five per cent of these freshmen will ever be graduated by the institution. We can estimate conservatively that instruction to freshmen who will eventually be graduated costs twice as much per student as does instruction to upper class students. Even more important than the dollar cost is the cost of the faculty's instructional time. In order to allow for transfers and scholarship drops during the freshman year, a publicly assisted institution must commit close to one-half of its available undergraduate instructional personnel and resources to providing classes for freshmen.

If we admit frankly that the freshman year is a time for surveying large blocks of knowledge and accumulating some basic intellectual tools, the locus of instruction during this year ought to be the automated library rather than the classroom. Admission to upper-division study can be determined by performance on standardized achievement tests administered whenever the student feels he has prepared himself sufficiently well. Aside from increased efficiency—think of the number of student contact hours that would be saved if the freshman year were eliminated—this program would more effectively provide for differences in idiosyncratic drive patterns than does our present system for freshman instruction.

A fourth curricular cornerstone is the course Fundamentals of Composition. The effectiveness of such a course for teaching students to write is open to some question. More importantly, demonstrations abound that students do not effectively transfer much of what they learn in this course to their writing efforts in other courses. It seems that removing this course from the curriculum entirely could easily effect a significant qualitative improvement. It might well be replaced by a program requiring at least one written assignment in every other course the student takes. Each of these assignments would be graded for style, composition, etc., by an English tutor who would meet individually with the writer to discuss the paper. This curricular change could be accomplished as cheaply as the present arrangement for teaching composition, and it has the virtue of encouraging a pervasive emphasis upon writing throughout the entire under-graduate curriculum.

Teaching Practices. Effective management of classroom learning, in the sense that I conceive it, requires teachers with advanced knowledge, skills, and certain attitudes toward human development and behavior as well as toward subject matter. The distressing fact is that college teachers have had little, if any, training in how learning can be managed. Whereas many are highly professional in their attitudes towards their scholarly disciplines, their responsibilities as catalysts for learning may be discharged superficially by assigning readings, meeting lectures, and administering some sort of examination for grading purposes.

In this section, I will first present a contrasting view of the way in which teachers *ought* to function; this will be followed by a suggestion about how they can be helped to function in this way.

How Should the Undergraduate Teacher Function? I envision the teacher as continuing to function as a manager of and catalyst for learning. In the world of my "druthers," I'd druther he'd do so more actively and deliberately than is now the case. If you step into this world with me, you will see him as a member of a "learning resources team." As a result of this team effort:

(1) Each student's previous attainments, cognitive development, and affective development will be continually monitored.

(2) Appropriate goals will be set for that student on the basis of the results of (1), above.

(3) A selection will be made from the full armamentarium of those instructional aids—including books, seminars, TV tapes, programs—that are best calculated to help the learner progress towards the goals set in (2), above.

How Can Teachers Be Helped to Function This Way? Two supporting all-university offices will be required to supplement each teacher's efforts. Along with the teacher, these offices will comprise the "learning resources team." One of these offices will be responsible for monitoring those student characteristics contributing to idiosyncratic drive patterns. It will collate all information available about each student's previous academic performance and periodically assess psychological characteristics known to be related to the differential effectiveness of alternative instructional settings.

The other all-university office will work closely with teachers, helping them to design instructional settings. In designing these settings, a rapprochement between the aims of the curriculum and the objectives of an isolated learning experience (or course) will have to be effected. In addition, no instructor can be expected to implement effectively an instructional setting that conflicts in serious ways with his own personal needs and gratifications.

Taken together, these two all-university offices will make it possible to optimize instruction for each student. One will guide the student into the instructional setting calculated to be most effective for him; the other will guide the instructor in establishing and maintaining a particular kind of instructional setting. This arrangement can be implemented most easily at the level where it is most necessary: in the first two undergraduate years of a four-year program. This is where registrations are largest, where multiple-section courses are the rule rather than the exception, and where academic mortality is the highest.

In brief, the plan will replace the presently unsystematic, irrational, and usually impersonal assignment of students to sections with one that is highly systematic, rational, and personal. Instead of allowing students to register for sections on the basis of a combination of intuition and what they hear on the campus grapevine, or alternatively, instead of permitting a computer to section on the basis of available student-stations at given hours, each student will be guided into particular sections because of his particular constellation of organismic characteristics.

Considering the other side of the coin, instead of playing it so much by ear, each teacher will be guided in conducting his section by a clear notion of the kind of instructional environment he is to provide and how he is to provide it. The plan can be implemented also in courses offered in only one section, but this will require even more sophisticated teachers. This is so because the teacher here will have to structure multiple learning experiences so that each one is optimal for a subset of his students. The "learning resources team" concept, however, is still applicable.

Two Final Questions. My interpretation of the implications of recent research on teaching and learning has led me to conclude that many curricular and instructional changes are needed. These suggested changes all stem from a single central premise: that higher education must be optimized for each learner.

We are left with two questions about the feasibility of attempts to optimize undergraduate instruction. The first concerns the matter of "technical feasibility." Do we know enough about the conditions of effective learning successfully to implement such programs? I am convinced that although we are far from knowing the whole story, we know enough to begin in these directions.

The second question concerns the matter of "strategic feasibility" or acceptability. Will college administrators and faculty members perceive such attempts as tenable in spite of the pressure of numbers to which they are continually subjected?

NOTES

1. L. Siegel, ed., *Instruction: Some Contemporary Viewpoints* (San Francisco: Chandler Publishing Co., 1967).

2. C. Rogers, "The Facilitation of Significant Learning," *ibid.*

3. E. Hilgard, ed., "Theories of Learning and Instruction," Part I, *Sixty-Third Yearbook of the National Society for the Study of Education* (Chicago: National Society for the Study of Education, 1964).

12

ARE OUR UNIVERSITIES SCHOOLS?

Henry C. Johnson, Jr.

Formerly a parish priest in the Episcopal Church, Henry C. Johnson, Jr. is now Assistant Professor of Education at Illinois State University, specializing in philosophy and history of education.

In surveying the noisy debate over higher educational strategy with which we are currently preoccupied, a careful observer can hardly escape the feeling that no real progress is being made. In spite of its scope and distinguished participants, the results of the debate appear to form no pattern of the sort from which thoughtful planning can issue. Growth and (as a consequence) change are facts. But the strange impasse which marks our efforts in the face of these phenomena, in the midst of vigorous discussion, suggests that some fundamental distinction has not been grasped with a clarity sufficient for the productive ordering of our critiques and proposals. Such, I believe, is the case; in this essay I shall attempt to delineate the missing distinction which seems at least in part to negate our attempted solutions.

Fundamental changes in our society in the past century have caused a new, historically unique intellectual institution to come into existence—the publicly maintained center for general and applied research and development. So gradually and unobtrusively has it come from the womb that we have been able to recognize its existence only negatively, in its effects, and particularly in the nearly fatal ambiguity which has been introduced into its academic birthplace. As a consequence of the birth of this New Institution, something is "wrong." But our "solutions" will be only transient or rhetorical until the existence of this New Institution is accepted as a primary principle of distinction, and is then consciously employed in alleviating our complex academic problems. Until it is so recognized, our analyses as well as our suggested improvements are doomed to work at cross-purposes.

The most significant fact about this New Institution, for our present purposes, is that its aim is not to be a school at all, at least in the traditional sense, but is rather, in large part, to solve the problems assigned to it by various agencies of our society and our nation, such as government, business, and particular professions. Our error has been to confuse radically the nature, criteria, and purposes of this New Institution with those of its matrix, the traditional school, and vice versa. The result of this mistake has been to becloud the question of whether we wish to continue the original institution at all, and to make it nearly impossible to develop sets of intelligent criteria which will apply precisely and fruitfully to each as a distinct institution. Because of the ambiguity inherent in our falsely unified category, we have faulted each for the other's mistakes and laid expectations upon the one which could be fulfilled only by the other. Slipping uncritically from one framework of analysis and discussion to the other, we have made productive judgment virtually impossible.*

THE NEW INSTITUTION

The roots of our confusion lie in history and sociology. Our customary institutional categories, such as family, state, and of course the school, have necessarily shaped our thinking; but in this case our uncritical acceptance of them has limited our ability to discern a fundamentally new situation.

The demands of our modern, revolutionary culture have forced a new intellectual institution into existence; but, since it

---

* A particularly forceful presentation of the effects of this failure, together with an even less optimistic prognosis, has been presented by Jacques Barzun under the title "The Liberal Arts Tradition Dead or Dying" in *The Intercollegian* of March, 1964.

has no exact historic parallel, it has been very difficult to recognize. It has consequently been nearly impossible for us to judge and criticize it, and hence to shape its growth and development. This New Institution is, as we have said, a new "intellectual" institution, but it is *sui generis*. It is a public center devoted primarily to research, analysis, and to some extent, specialized training.

From this very loose preliminary definition a number of crucial subsidiary distinctions follow. The school, then, is no longer the only intellectual institution in our culture, nor is the only intellectual vocation that of the traditional scholar-teacher. What has confused us is the fact that the New Institution is *like* the school. But "like" is not, of course, "the same." It is *like* the school only insofar as its work is largely intellectual. Further confusion stems from the fact that the New Institution is also *like* a commercial institution in that it has certain limited tasks to accomplish, certain assigned problems to solve. Its potential range is, however, far broader and not specified by restricted motives. The source of its unique nature and purpose is the fact that the scientific-industrial revolution has made it impossible for a nation to survive without the services of publicly maintained centers of thought, research, and intellectual praxis as focal points and resource centers for certain kinds of decisions. Because of the "partnership" approach to social problems, these New Institutions logically have come to be publicly organized but privately subsidized and utilized.

This New Institution has no exact historical parallel and it needs none. What it does need is not to be confused with anything but itself, to be free from judgments based upon an attractive, but entirely erroneous, simile relating to an accident of its birth. The problem is that this generically new intellectual institution has grown up in the shell of the traditional academic structure. Having now reached a kind of early maturity, as an independently viable organism, separation from this shell is required or we risk the danger of destroying both. For the New Institution to continue to be garbed in an academic frock is anomalous, to say the least. The whole business is as unnecessary and ridiculous as it would be to suppose that towns which grew up around ancient abbeys or cathedrals ought to have deans or abbots as their principal officials, or that their public servants ought to wear cassocks.

The fact that we have not noticed with sufficient clarity this New Institution's growing up in and through the traditional academic form has introduced the ambiguity into the debate over the contemporary academic institution. Recognizing the true situation (that we have been discussing not one institution but two) will serve both to make understandable many of the problems that have caused us so much trouble and provide a basis for genuinely effective thought about both. Perhaps most important of all, its use can save us from entirely losing sight of the other critically important intellectual institution, the school or educational community.

We have gone, of course, some way toward employing our distinction. On the positive side, institutions like the National Institute of Health or the Los Alamos community represent certain, very rudimentary examples of this new kind of institution, but they are far too limited in their conception to satisfy the larger public need. Likewise, perceptive critics of American higher learning, specifically men such as Robert Hutchins and Jacques Barzun, have drawn our attention to the negative force of a developing technology on American educational life. But their solutions have not pleased us. Thinkers of otherwise indubitable perspicacity, like Veblen for example, struggled continually (and needlessly) either to deny legitimacy to one function or the other, or to force one or the other function into that institutional model they thought superior. We have rightly if ignorantly resisted their insistence on our choosing which we *preferred*. On a sounder analysis no such Hobson's choice is required.

We must also recognize the obvious fact that the modern "university" cannot be salvaged by rhetorical devices. It is not a "multiversity" or anything else of the sort: it is not a university at all, in the traditional sense; and it does us no good at all to define it by an educationally bowdlerized label. The modern "university" does not even bear a genuine likeness to the traditional one. Its only common bond is that of employing some of the traditional terms, ideals, and organizational schemata, and the possession of a thoroughly corrupted version of its long-standing (but still socially neccessary) educative function. It is simply no longer principally a school. Furthermore, I judge that it no longer "should" be, *provided* we recognize that now that the child has come to overshadow the parent, we are left virtually bereft of adequate educational institutions at the highest level, and *provided* that we proceed at once to rectify this situation. Our persistence in trying to exemplify whatever symbolic bonds remain can only be fatally harmful to both. The cord must be cut, though this is not meant to imply that the association of the two intellectual communities is either unprofitable or impossible. It means only that the confusion of the two communities will do justice to neither.

Historically, we might have seen the present dilemma as implicit in the Morrill Acts and the rise of the "land-grant" colleges. Understandably, our mistake was to assume too uncritically that we were merely adding a new *dimension* to higher educational responsibility, as the apology so often runs, when we were in fact posing a solution for a new demand in our culture: sophisticated public intellectual direction in areas which far transcended the capacity of educational institutions. Since, in the beginning, the demand was seen and interpreted minimally, we could carry on for a while on the basis of the "new dimension" approach. But the subsequent proliferation of demands has increasingly forced us to see that a new idea, a wholly new kind of institution, was really involved. That such an institution, lacking in historic parallels, went unrecognized need not cause us undue chagrin, unless of course, we should persist in failing to take cognizance of it.

The development implicit in the "land-grant" colleges actually preceded the German university "ideal" which was later appropriated as an apology for the research complex by then coming on strongly. Doubtless the "German ideal" was sometimes stressed for its own virtues, but probably it was a justification of the new "educational" apparatus as well. To equate what we are now doing, however, with the "German ideal" would be a bit silly, even if it were not already directly harmful. In spite of the emotional exhortations of the Flexners and the Harpers, we no longer have it, though we may have preserved some of its worst anachronisms—captivity to national ends, rigid specialization, and so on. In any case, our enormously overdeveloped academic complexes should no longer be justified or analyzed after this model, if, indeed, they ever should have been.

The point is, simply, that the functions and the criteria of these New Institutions are no longer educative ones. That is, they are not chiefly concerned with providing a critically maintained intellectual tradition and the basic skills necessary for employing it and effectively placing it at the disposal of our citizenry. The immediate practical problem, then, comes down to this: We must choose whether we wish to turn the present "university" entirely into the New Institution, without cramping it by an educative mold, and then build anew along properly educational lines—or whether we wish to restore strictly educational functions to our present centers of higher learning and build the New Institution separately.

PROBLEMS PRECIPITATED BY THE NEW INSTITUTION

It will be useful now to examine briefly a few of the specific problems which have arisen from the birth of the New Institution within the traditional one. This examination should also help clarify the distinction we have been trying to develop.

First of all, we shall examine the effect of our distinction upon the problems of size and the respective roles of government and business. It has been understandably profitless to compare sizes, and the advantages of size, between institutions which have not in fact been comparable, which are not even generally similar—as would be the case in discussing the function and merits of size at, say, Dartmouth and the University of California. Similarly, it is obvious that we are ill-advised to debate the effect of government aid at M.I.T. and Ripon College as if those effects were even capable of comparison, let alone quite the same. One is a traditional college, the other our current hybrid—The New-Institution-*cum*-educational-appendage. To attempt to compare them is merely to compound the confusion. For example, private or governmental capital invested on a necessarily elaborate scientific apparatus or a program of research at Berkeley will not be likely to induce either a conservative or a socialistic bias in its freshmen. On the other hand, an imprecise distinction will probably fail to suggest the real force that enormous subsidization can have in pushing a purportedly *educational* institution into research and development which is biased, *educationally* speaking. The sort of subsidization which is now widely encouraged assuredly does give undue weight and prestige to certain kinds of questions, questions which are raised and selected for consideration in accordance with an essentially *non*educational principle. Indeed, all the queries about productivity or educational effectiveness become hopelessly entangled when put isomorphically to the entire range of American higher "education," from our vast "universities" to our humble community "colleges." *

Next, we must focus our attention on some internal problems. Take first the case of that benighted "central figure" in the academic world, the professor. We have worried with him of late over his status. But, as a matter of fact, a conflict which touches his very identity has followed from our confusion of the two institutions. Frequently—indeed, nearly always—he has been educated as a teacher, that is, in the traditional pattern. Should he attempt to remain such (an unlikely possibility if he has any "get-up-and-go," we say), he will be at least partially corrupted, for the criteria utilized in advancing him (or retaining him at all) will be those drawn from the New Institution. He will be required to be a "productive scholar," but "productive" will be interpreted almost exclusively as "advancing" knowledge in a particular mode whose relevance is stipulated usually from a particular problem-centered viewpoint. If he desires the *super-*

---

* This discussion raises one point which must be kept clearly in mind both here and throughout the balance of this essay. My aim is not to defend the "good" humanistic, liberal-arts tradition from absorption by the "bad" scientifically-oriented "multiversity," "megaversity," or whatever one wishes to call it. Of course, the debate has become so blindly acrimonious that it will be almost impossible for that disclaimer to be accepted. Each side will doubtless see me as a captive of the other. The all-important consideration is that both will suffer without need or profit if this distinction is not carefully made.

additum, the "real" prestige, it will be his solely through engaging "useful"—that is, publicly relevant—questions, now more and more assigned to him by government and industry directly. (The staggering growth and peculiar force of such prestige in itself powerfully testifies to the validity of this analysis.) Now, if the professor cannot do this, possibly because his particular expertise does not lend itself to such immediate employment, he will probably attempt something much worse: By a flurry of activity and trivial writing, he will try to look as if he can be so valued. Our "learned journals" and our Sunday editions are already groaning with attempts to appear valuable, attempts which would profit by a bit of leisurely steeping. One might be inclined to be angry were it not for the fact that the annual summary of the department's "productivity" haunts the road ahead for so many of these folk.

We have also wondered why the professor's allegiance (so necessary to an educational community) is less and less to his alma mater and more and more, say, to the American Chemical Society, the Department of Defense, or the Du Pont Corporation. The answer is obvious. Furthermore, for the new-model practitioner, teaching often becomes merely a way of gaining and employing neophytes for the New Institution rather than a compelling vocation for educating in its own right. Genuine scholars have no time for it (if they are "really" productive) or no inclination for it, since their heady, if inflated, status depends upon satisfying misapplied criteria uncritically borrowed from those which ought to characterize the New Institution. Yet the fact remains that teachers—genuine, full-time teachers, whose research is for the purpose of enlivening their teaching and not necessarily solving problems posed by others—are an absolute necessity in an educational institution. Their status would also be high if their vocation could be kept properly distinct and if it were not judged by terms drawn unconsciously from the wrong conceptual framework.

By the same token, the prestige disciplines are of necessity those whose honor is primarily externally derived. As was the case with the professor, comparisons are particularly odious when they are unconsciously shifted from one universe of dis-

course to another. So long as we retain our confusion between
the New Institution and an institution dedicated to education,
we cannot justify Latin and English Literature without at least a
trace of embarrassment, particularly before the general public.
The public's lack of distinct criteria, which makes it almost
impossible for them to accord true status to the teacher, also
obstructs their accepting programs which "waste time" instead
of getting the job done. In fact, it becomes exceedingly difficult
to rule any disciplinary area in or out of the institution's proper
sphere of responsibility with a clear conscience. Our frame of
reference for defining both prestige and utility shifts between a
rather narrow, present-centered practicality and general education; thus any subject can be made to appear either wise or
foolish: Latin doesn't "help" chemistry; chemistry does not give
"broad" education by itself. Where there is no stable principle
of exclusion, argument can hardly proceed. One of the results of
this dilemma is that the "university" operates most clearly like
an educational institution in the "unproductive" fields, such as
literature and philosophy. But in these areas the problem arises
that the general prestige of such pursuits declines as a whole;
and, because of the mixed judgments which are necessarily
made, there is little opportunity to raise the stock of such fields
with the layman.

From the preceding observations the proposal might be inferred that the New Institution be given responsibility for the
sciences and that the traditional institution keep the arts. Nothing could be further from the truth. Just what the New Institution will embrace needs no artificial distinctions such as liberal,
artistic, valuational, or the like. Its tasks do not arise from trying
to form men or convey a broad tradition, but from solving
problems which face the culture, in fact or in theory. We can
clearly see that the New Institution would embrace all the
natural, social, and behavioral sciences, and technological problems as well. What such institutions could or would accomplish,
even in areas previously restricted to an exclusively academic
arts approach, is something about which we can only speculate
for the present. The traditional educational institution clearly
would retain science, but as an activity qualified by *educative*

criteria. How scientists think and function, what they have thought and discovered, as it shapes men and societies, is naturally to be included. The school, however, is not a place for the practice of science in the full sense of that word, any more than it is the appropriate locus for the practice of drama as a vocation. It cannot be. The fact that most schools now physically resemble great factories or industrial research facilities is as anomalous as the fact that a few years ago technological machinery had to be hidden behind ivy-covered Gothic walls. Form has followed function; but that is a sounder canon for architecture than it is for education. It is no more preferable that industrial plant design or organization should coerce the natural and essentially communal life of an educational institution than that research centers should have stained glass windows and faculty clubs.

Our being fooled into thinking that the contemporary "university" has education as its chief purpose has also led us to assume that quality education could only take place in such institutions. This assumption has cost the "small colleges" dearly; it may even have cost us their invaluable contribution. We have looked at our educationally deceiving monsters and said, "Now that's the place where people really get a schooling. Count up the advantages in terms of men, machines, books, etc." By comparison with Michigan and Cal. Tech., Williams and Lawrence can look anemic indeed—but only when the proper criteria are misapplied. The educative function of the large university has declined shockingly, as anyone who has faced a bored graduate instructor or stared into a flickering closed-circuit telecast can testify. Why argue about it? The small college, provided that it is alive to its proper function, can educate and can educate very well indeed. What it cannot do is compete as a center for public intellectual practice.

The point is, of course, that both institutions are desperately needed; confused imitations of either will be fatal. Community, identity, purpose: these are virtues in educational institutions. They may have some application to the new-model intellectual center also, but they will be defined in quite different ways. Skilled teachers, alive to ideas and issues, can prepare people for taking their place in research, or in other walks of life; they cannot be this, nor can they do more than equip (with a "prayer," if you will, that the spirit also catches) for the intelligent and continually educative life that should lie ahead for any human being. And, they surely cannot make this invaluable contribution if their very existence is jeopardized by their lack of research contracts or the absence of large-scale computers from their properly peaceful environs. Most of us persist in so faulting them, in spite of the fact that it has not yet been demonstrated that machines make education. Before we consign our structure of genuinely educational institutions to oblivion, and concentrate on doubling and redoubling our present amorphous institutions, we ought to understand what we are in danger of doing.

We have already suggested rather strongly that the virtues, symbols, and structures of an academic institution are not necessarily those of a competitive intellectual workshop, and vice versa. It may perhaps be useful to reinforce the point once more, this time in a particular area. Virtually every school is shredded today by excessive departmentalization and specialization, and by the vast management problems occasioned by a proliferation of institutes, service projects and special programs. Organization of the sort suited to achieve effective concentration and specialization is of the essence in "task force" work, but it is also the bane of wholesome education. Arguing about which is to obtain in the "super-school" is a thorough waste of time. A careful distinction between our institutions can free us from the whole business. What we cannot do is to insist that either form must characterize the other, or that an irrational *mélange* characterize a "single" institution, which is now irreparably broken underneath its academic façade.

A similar confusion leads us to assume that large-scale education is more efficient and economically preferable. Large-scale research and problem-solving may be, but the notion is, at the very least, dubious in reference to education.* It is surely time

---

* It is perhaps worth noting that even some large industries have been moving rapidly toward decentralization for precisely this reason: to promote the identity and the motivation of their most highly skilled and creative personnel.

that someone, perhaps one of the ever-beneficent foundations, calculated the true cost (in terms of time and money) of, for example, making a vital *educational* decision in our larger institutions of "higher learning." Flexibility, outwardly so apparent in the vast array of special interests, is in reality incredible rigidity when it comes to such crucial educational decisions as curriculum development, student guidance, and so on. While we may have learned to move with the ease of a leopard technologically, educationally our bulk has reduced us to the state of a woolly mammoth.

Another result of our failure to distinguish the two institutions we now require, and to value them both in appropriate terms, is the problem of curriculum mentioned above. Course content, even for undergraduates, has tended to get structured more and more according to its specialized use, professionally and not educationally. The minute and arbitrary divisions, possibly productive of "scholarship," which characterize many history offerings might serve as a case in point. Frequently they mark only the divisions of competence which are realistic for the historical researcher, faced as he is with more and more data to be examined. Less and less frequently do they represent valid vehicles for acquiring a general conception of history. General education then becomes an almost insuperable problem: For his requirement in "History," should Mr. X. take a course covering twenty-five years of modern French history, or one involving two hundred years of ancient history? What obviously needs to be done by the practitioner of history obviously interferes with virtually any grasp of general history by the learner. Nor can we base our hopes on the notion that the insight of "doing" history gained by sitting at the feet (now frequently at cable's length) of a great historian will automatically carry over in the individual's way of life. When pressed, professor and student alike know that this is simply a very bad joke, one at which they might laugh, were its consequences not so dire!

The form and magnitude of our "educational" institutions prevent resolution of problems of intellectual breadth through the association of faculty and students—that is, through the communal aspects which have previously characterized the best education. We all recognize that in institutions numbering their members in the tens of thousands some smaller unit of distribution is imperative, both administratively and psychologically. One of the most obvious ways to accomplish this (and also perhaps one of the most dangerous, educationally speaking) is by trade lines. Virtually every department—jealous gods indeed!—rushes to isolate its neophytes, if possible into physically distinct areas. A tragically narrowing regimen follows: the student's books, his living quarters, and even where he drinks his coffee and eats his lunch often become carefully circumscribed. In the name of identity and productivity, literary men need not stumble over educators; physicists need not suffer poets or artists. Through this chastening discipline, the optimum state is achieved: Vocational segregation, enhanced by economic segregation in the social sphere, virtually assures the student (and even the faculty member) that he need not encounter anyone who might informally broaden his viewpoint.

The previous consideration leads naturally into a more careful look at two other figures of central importance in the educational world, the president and the student. The academic president is torn asunder by this confusion of images. His desire for resignation—in the administrative sense, not the spiritual—and his frequent cries of anguish make this abundantly clear. Could a more discerning analysis relieve his schizoid condition? Because of the confusion we have been attempting to delineate, he is expected to be what no one man can be: an administrator of a vast intellectual-industrial empire, a fund-raiser for an apparatus too large to appeal to anybody, and a folksy ceremonial officer and "end-of-the-log" educator. The New Institution calls for an administrator, period. Its finances can and should be justified and secured on their own peculiar grounds and from their appropriate sources. The school demands a leader of a faculty and possibly even a leader of students (though that we shall ever see that day again is probably more of a hope than a certainty, even if reforms come). On one occasion, I had the opportunity to meet socially a deservedly famous "educator" and university president on the day that one of his faculty members had disgraced himself and his profession because of his involvement in a nationally publicized scandal. This particular president remarked sadly and wistfully that he thought it was too bad; he had never met the man, but he had heard that he was really very good. Any normal person is shocked and offended by that. Why? Because knowing one's faculty is important, whether one is a president or a professor, in an educational institution. One would not, on the other hand, be shocked to learn that the board chairman of a vast corporation did not know his supervisor of parts-replacement. Nor should we be outraged at this particular president, inasmuch as it is our policy that has forced him to grow more like the latter than the former. The trouble is that we are still trying to cling to a terminology and symbolism which tries quite unsuccessfully to make us think he is or can be both board chairman and president.

The man at the other end of the educational log is equally confused and confusing. The student is, of course, the one chiefly victimized by the growth of our "megaversities," though he is usually the last of our concerns. Paradoxically, the university has frighteningly complicated the search for the purpose and identity it is supposed to support.

The truth of this is so obvious that we can pass on to the less commonly discussed fact that the student presents a confusing appearance to the outsider as well. The "man-in-the-street" assumes that formal education ought not to go on forever; he is suspicious of the "student's" unduly prolonging the luxury of schooling. The fact is, however, that the professionally involved graduate student is not by any means wholly a student. He is also a productive worker in the New Institution; and, were it not for our prevalent confusion, he would be viewed and treated as such. Silly academic degree programs, tuition charges, and the rest of the traditional university carryover, should simply be scrapped. Instead, he should be a paid worker, a new kind of public servant who is learning as a modern-day apprentice in the new intellectual complex, but also doing something entirely relevant to the public good. For the "student" to structure his life, emotionally and financially, as a student, irritated rather than broadened by the symbolic attempt to give him more "general" education (through such things as "minors" in other fields and some of the less useful language requirements) is a

pitiful if not harmful gesture. It should fool no one, least of all
the student, though it sometimes does.

One alternative to this anonymity coupled with frustration
—and one open to the student on his own initiative—is sheer
rebellion in any of a number of areas. The fact that students
are beginning to act out this alternative with rather distaste-
ful results and with widespread publicity frightens us just
a little. Such rebellions, with or without substantial issues as
warrants, are made even more dangerous when, as becomes
obvious, neither the administration nor the faculty have any real
communication with the participants. When the breakdown actually takes place as it did at the University of California in
1964, the whole business comes to resemble (no matter how
unfairly) nothing so much as a labor-management dispute in a
company town. A clear-cut distinction between education and
the practice of the new intellectual vocation might alleviate
considerably both the student's frustrations and the institution's
problems. And, it should go without saying, the distinction
would be of the greatest value in marking out the areas of
responsible freedom, not simply to increase the student's docil-
ity.

What then, is the immediate strategy to be? Clearly, this is a
question which cannot receive full discussion here. However,
our distinction implies that any realistic strategy should have
certain defining characteristics, which can be stated in three
words: separation, federation, incorporation. Very simply put,
the first step is this: to proceed to establish our public centers of
research and development in their own right, and at the same
time to re-establish effective educational institutions in their own
right as well. Organize, administer, and finance the New Institution without the claptrap of degrees and gowns and pathetic
attempts at "general education." Free it for the most effective
pursuit of its perfectly valid purposes, and through the means
judged most efficient by the relevant criteria. On the other hand,
we must also organize, administer, and finance educational institutions, with faculties composed of teachers, with executives
who are educators, and with courses of study which are structured educationally and not in terms of a bogus "productivity"

that is not theirs to give. We should still expect teachers to stay "alive," but as teachers, and not as new model public intellectual practitioners. We would still hope that the problems tackled in the New Institutions would be posed in the education of all, and their results incorporated by educational institutions into all curricula which purport to educate. No one, in short, can argue for a stifling separation; what we can hope for is an intelligent and fruitful integration. But it must be an integration based on acceptance of the fact that our present universities have ceased to be schools.

In the second place, recognizing the essentially destructive effects of unregulated size which have been forced upon us by the growth of the New Institution, we should frankly face the issue and create small colleges. The reasons for creating intentionally limited institutions are principally two: to insure at least the possibility of the communal life so important in education, and to permit a broadly representative faculty which is still sufficiently manageable to participate as a whole in the formation of educational methods and goals. Now, whereas artificially limiting size might create a stifling and ingrown atmosphere if done in isolation, a federation of such colleges, in healthy competition on the basis of educational effectiveness rather than size, could probably avoid this pitfall. Furthermore, given such a basic strategy, membership in the constellation of educational institutions could include private colleges as well. Their inclusion seems essential if we are to avoid the monochromatic kind of education which too easily results from exclusively public control.

Finally, we cannot avoid the fact that the apparatus of inquiry, libraries, machines, and special programs of many sorts, is now so complicated and expensive that it cannot be duplicated at random. As a consequence, many of the best minds must perforce assemble about that apparatus. We have argued that while education is properly distinct from either pure or applied research, no false isolation from them is either feasible or profitable. As a consequence, the best strategy might be to incorporate our federated colleges around these complexes, though taking great pains to guard the independence and the proper image of the former. In this fashion, the major resources could be drawn upon for educational ends, communication would not be so likely to break down, and the joint functions of building and advancing the total intellectual life of our society could be cooperatively pursued.

13

THE PROBLEM OF LEADERSHIP IN THE UNIVERSITY

Ross L. Mooney

Ross L. Mooney is Professor of Education at the Ohio State University. He was a member of the staff of the Bureau of Educational Research from 1938 to 1965. His journal articles number over one hundred in such areas as college personnel and administration, education of the disadvantaged, and creative behavior.

I present seventeen propositions concerning the leadership situation in the modern large university. These propositions were derived from a study of one institution; the results of that study are reworded into propositions so that they might stand as challenges useful to others in the appraisal of their own situations and views.

The propositions fall into three sets, the first relating to a split in the university community between teaching and research, the second relating to fundamental shifts inside the university since 1900, and the third relating directly to the leadership situation.

The propositional form allows me to convert my observations of one situation into a frame of reference by which other men may check their own views. It is not important that others agree with me; what *is* important is that every university open its eyes to the reality of its situation, whatever that reality may be. Leadership is a crucial problem.

PROPOSITIONS RELATING TO THE SPLIT BETWEEN TEACHING AND RESEARCH

PROPOSITION 1

Present-day research is a new development having its own special roots; powerful precedents have been set by the way in which research has been financed in the country since the war.

When contracting agencies of government or industry have given money for research, they have stipulated the categories within which the proposals may be offered and have reserved to themselves the power to accept or reject each specific proposal. When Congress sets up money for research, it stipulates the categories in which money can be spent and sets up its own specific agencies to pass on the specific proposals submitted. When the state legislature gives money to the university for research, it, too, stipulates the categories in which the money is to be spent. Private foundations use the same pattern of thought. All along the line, the precedent has been set that those who have the money have the power to control the specific research which they purchase.

These recent precedents do not include arrangements for using outside money to back the universities as such for what their professors, out of their own wisdom and experience, shall name as good research to be doing. The universities have been by-passed as agencies adequate in their own right to determine what research to do. They are seen by outside agencies as pools of people available for use as these agencies see fit.

PROPOSITION 2

Responding over a number of years to these precedents in financing research, we have accepted them as valid for determining how we should administer our own funds when we are free, within the university, to do as we wish.

To administer "free money for research," we set up central university committees to which we give the power to approve specific proposals. Administration is not through the regular lines of the budget (i.e., president, deans, department chairmen, faculty members) but through committees, authorized by the faculty to operate out of the office of the president.

Control by these committees is absolute. Though the university might have viewed these groups as responsible for the legislation of principles and policies, leaving the responsibility for judgment and administration of specifics to normal channels of authority, the university has not done so. It has given the committees total power—legislative, judicial, and executive.

Faculty members who obtain help for their research, whether through local committees or outside agencies, therefore do so by special channels, separated from their normal departmental routes. Department heads and deans, though they see the papers passing through, tend to become spectators of a separate operation in which they have no crucial part. Department heads tend to restrict their views of themselves to that of being supervisors of arrangements for teaching, letting research become what it will as individual faculty members are motivated and controlling committees decide. A coordinator of research, acting for a dean at the college level, becomes little more than a communicative agent, serving between two poles of power, one held by the individual faculty member who has the power of initiative and the other by the agency which has the power of specific approval. Neither department heads nor deans have real leadership potential in this matter, nor realistic capacity to assume responsibility for the integral functioning of the university activity.

PROPOSITION 3

Two systems are developing, side by side, in the university, one for the normal lines of budgeting and responsibility centering on teaching, and the other for special agencies and operations centering on research.

The former is embedded in the historical and philosophic tradition of the university as an agency independent of all others, free and responsible for its own evaluations; the latter is embedded in a newer perspective of the university as dependent on other agencies and responsible for serving their interests.

The split shows up in a number of ways. The word "research" is becoming attached to the kind of inquiry a man can get special allocations of money to do. The tendency now is to conclude that a man is not doing research if he does not have special money to do it. The vitality of inquiry as an essential ingredient to the efforts of professors in *all* university disciplines is weakened as the spotlight goes to those who have the special funds.

Research becomes a game of specialization, specialization in knowing the particular frame of mind of particular committees and agencies, and specialization in knowing the kind of research which these bodies regard as good. As money flows from the bigger agencies into the research they value, the research which is produced increases so sharply in volume that ever more specialization is needed just to keep up to date in the rapidly moving field. Full-time attention is needed by increasing numbers of staff, relieved of other university operations for research work.

With research focusing on the concretions of specific projects and specific men, the definition of what is "good" in research shifts inside the university from a more generalized meaning applying to all university disciplines to a more restricted meaning derived from the characteristics of the projects and men; and, the definition of what is "good" in research (inside the university) comes vividly to light in the way the central university committee behaves when passing judgment on the specific proposals submitted to it.

Individuals from a wide variety of disciplines make up the committee. Faced with the necessity of passing judgment on proposals from a score or more of different disciplines, the individual members quickly sense their personal incapacity to make judgments about proposals in those fields in which they have no professional authority themselves. As men who want to be fair and just, and who are sensitive to the criticism of colleagues whom they may have to turn down, they come under great pressure to find a consistent operating procedure which makes them as safe as possible. The line of safety is evidently found in agreement among themselves that all projects shall follow what is currently called "good methodology."

Perspective on "good methodology" derives from pooled experience in the bulk of research in the university. Since World War II, this experience has come through contract research, emphasizing technology and the natural sciences. When committee members are faced with research proposals which are humanistically or holistically oriented—as much research in the social sciences, humanities, and arts necessarily needs to be— they do not see the "good methodology" they are looking for in their safety zone; they feel inept and uncertain, and vote negatively. Certain areas in the university community, therefore, suffer while the areas which have had the most support from outside funds to date tend, again, to be the ones to receive favor in the eyes of the central university committee.

In this way, the values of agencies outside the university have come to dominate the values of the university itself. We are being led by outside money; we do not adequately maintain and assert our integrity as university men directly responsible for wise and balanced leadership of the minds and values of men. We have abrogated our responsibilities even when we have had the chance to accept them in the administration of our self-controlled funds.

We have come to a situation where the integrity of the university enterprise is being challenged in the value splits which modern pressures have introduced and which we, more unconsciously than consciously, have further supported by our own policies.

PROPOSITION 4

Our willingness to go along on the split between teaching and research is understandable in the light of several contributing conditions inside the university and out: academic status of research, competition from outside the university, inflation, service in the cold war, costly research in the technologies, public

acclaim, inflationary enrollments, research specialization, interdepartmental financing of research,
precedent from gifts, and the recently heightened value
of the good teacher.

(1) The academic tradition implies that every professor
should be a research man and that highest status in the university is to be given to those men who turn out the most or best
research; promotions are used to support this policy; research
has a prime value.

(2) In industry and government, new opportunities are being
offered for full-time research without teaching; this offers both
competition and a model for the complete separation of research
and teaching.

(3) In an inflationary economy, with lagging pay scales,
faculty members need supplementary income; outside research
money offers that opportunity.

(4) Money for contract research is often tied to loudly pro-
claimed and genuine needs of the nation for survival in a cold
war world; doing such research is an obvious service to the
nation and thereby personally satisfying in ways competing with
personal satisfactions from teaching.

(5) Much research is quite expensive, particularly in technological lines where national interests are most obviously focused;
special funds, set aside specifically for given work, are necessary
to get the research done.

(6) Many faculty members who, heretofore, found themselves unheralded outside the cloisters of the university now find
themselves wanted in the big world beyond. Having been taught
by the general culture in America that whoever joins a university staff does so knowing that he thereby sacrifices all right to
the prospect of general public acclaim for the possible acclaim
of his esoteric group, many a professor now sees that he can
have both university acclaim *and* general public acclaim; how
good!

(7) Inflationary enrollments put pressures on faculty members to increase their teaching loads; faculty members need

obvious protection against such pressures in order to do research; project administration of research provides that protection.

(8) Fields of knowledge are rapidly increasing in complexity; specialization in research is often necessary at a level beyond that which can be readily shared with undergraduate or graduate students; protection for research beyond teaching usage is necessary and available in project packaging.

(9) Since much research is now interdepartmental, the traditional line of financing by departments no longer works. Project financing provides flexibility to fit interdepartmental situations.

(10) The first moneys for research have been gifts in which the donors could feel satisfaction if they could see the specific results of their donations; specific research projects allow the donors this satisfaction. The same precedent serves for contract research.

(11) Income from gifts and "profits" from contract research have been too small to amount to anything worthwhile if distributed over the full range of departments and faculty members; project administration of research money avoids the problem of fruitless scattering.

(12) Although research, by tradition, is highly valued, teaching is also highly valued; as enrollment pressures increase, as fields of knowledge become more complex, as curriculum problems become more severe, and as research men leave teaching to do separated research work, the good teacher becomes a freshly valued man; in this line of reaction, some administrators and some teachers now choose to put higher value on teaching than on research; the split between teaching and research becomes an open and contentious issue, with defenders on both sides.

Many conditions, inside the university and out, are therefore contributing to the split between teaching and research.

Further conditions contribute to splittings in the university community, evident in the story of what has happened to power in the university community in the course of this century. Fundamental shifts of power have occurred since 1900.

PROPOSITION 5

Power to integrate the internal operations of the university, according to tradition, is lodged within the assembled faculty; the tradition is based on an era which is no longer dominant.

Tradition grants power to the faculty of a university to design the operation of the internal affairs of the university. The professors are seen as professional men who, like other professional men, are given freedom and responsibility to make their own judgments of what to do. They are not subservient to any other agency; their discipline derives from their professional ethics and their common loyalty to the general welfare. A board of trustees is necessary to provide a channel for support from society, but the board's power over money is not to be used as power to control its substantive use in the academic program. The latter is the responsibility of the faculty.

This tradition was established in American higher education well before 1900. Institutions were then small. (The average size of the twenty universities having the largest staff was 255 in 1901.) It was psychologically feasible to vest power in the faculty working as an assembled body. The individual faculty member, in the normal range of his daily experience, could be expected to confront the diversity of interrelated problems with which the institution was faced. When seated with the assembled faculty to make an institutional decision, he could honor the integrity of institutional operation by virtue of his capacity to render holistic judgments, foreseeing the multiple consequences of potential decisions on varied aspects of the university. The faculty could see itself functioning as a community and could operate as one because its individual members could comprehend the totality within their concrete personal experience.

With legislative and judicial functions carried out by faculty assembly, the executive and leadership functions could be carried out by personalities cast in the role of representatives of the faculty. Department chairmen could be clearly perceived as chairmen, responsible to their departmental staffs for fulfilling the faculty group's expectations. The university president could be construed as the faculty man whose business it was to fend for the faculty when facing the world beyond the campus. The community was small enough to make personal acquaintance-ship possible among most of its members so that those given leadership posts could be seen as persons personally responsible for the welfare of one another in the total communal enterprise. Authority was given by the group; neither specialization of function nor other separation was then sufficient to put administrators in a class apart from the personal and direct claims of the individuals in the group. The rules of the game were those of a personally responsive morality.

In such a cultural context, the image of the university as an institution-run-by-its-faculty was born and consolidated into the lore of higher education. Faculty members, not being granted top status by those in the broader society, could in this way claim top spot for themselves in a community run by them-selves. To this image was attached a series of rationalizations about the sanctity of the academic function in a society, aimed at preserving the virtue of the university-in-its-own-right, re-gardless of the projections of a society upon it. Within this body of rationalizations, the professor could assure himself of his own virtue whether society has the good grace to acknowledge it or not.

PROPOSITION 6

The faculty, today, faces a world beyond the campus which has undergone profound changes and which has brought about consequent changes inside the uni-versity.

The world has undergone war, depression, war, and an uneasy peace. It has proliferated a powerful technology, realign-ing values of education according to need for advancing training in new occupations. New professions have become necessary as complexity of the social and intellectual order has accompanied the complexity of economic production and consumption. As

the people have changed in their needs and in their perceptions
of preparation for life in the modern world, the universities have
changed from small to large, from simple to complex.

Since World War II, these changes have accelerated at a
nearly exhausting pace. In the private speech of conscientious
leaders of higher education, a deeply plaintive note now commonly appears as they struggle to gain commanding perspective
and intelligent control of what is happening inside their institutions. This note of plaintiveness derives from a feeling not only
of having gotten behind in the game, but perhaps of having lost
the ball altogether.

PROPOSITION 7

The university has lost access to a center of responsive
power.

What was formerly taken as a clear center of power—i.e., the
assembled faculty—is no longer an effective instrument for
making institutional decisions. It is too big, too diverse. (The
average size of the twenty universities having the largest staff
was 2,020 in 1958.) If the faculty were assembled, its individuals would not be sufficiently holistic in their experience of the
total situation to be able to judge with confidence the best
course to take in many, if not most, of the situations presented.

In lieu of government by the total faculty, by a series of
accretions several smaller faculty units have evolved to carry out
specific responsibilities of the institution. Typically, a university
has a sizable faculty council, made up of representatives of the
academic staff, to take up the prerogatives formerly held by the
total faculty assembly. Feeding into this council are a number of
subcouncils, manned by appointive and ex-officio personnel who
take responsibility for monitoring different major functions of
the university. Chief among these are councils on instruction,
research, off-campus services, athletics, and graduate affairs.
Subordinate in the total complex are still further councils, committees, boards, and institutes (e.g., library councils, committees
on student discipline, admission boards, institutes for research).

Such units overlay or cross through the traditional colleges, schools, bureaus, experiment stations, and departments. As these varied agencies of academic power act, further agencies arc of course necessary to carry action into daily operation. The traditional administrative offices of president, deans, and department chairmen, largely adequate for administration in 1900, are no longer adequate. New offices, centers, and services are needed. These tend to be grouped according to major functions of university operation, being formed into such areas as curriculum, research, and public relations. Manning these units are vice-presidents, executive heads, personnel deans, directors, and supervisors. In large universities, mere naming of the university's legislative and administrative agencies and their personnel can take twenty pages in a campus directory.

PROPOSITION 8

With academic power and operational responsibility divided and subdivided, again and again, the image of the university as an integral community progressively dissipates.

Faculty members tend to surrender their responsibility for an integral community. They turn over to student personnel offices the responsibility for guidance, counseling, and care of the students, retaining the teaching and grading of students on work done in their courses and feeling that these activities now fulfill a sufficient obligation to students. To curriculum committees they turn over the responsibility for making sense out of curricular patterns, feeling that, as individuals, they lack the information necessary really to know what makes sense for the students beyond the limits of courses in their particular areas. To the council on research and related bodies, they turn over the responsibility for designing the administration of research activity in the university, feeling their individual interests are met if they can but know the lines by which they may submit their own research proposals. To the university office for long-range planning, they turn over the large responsibility for designing the university of the future; this problem is much too large and complex to hope for personal mastery, given the work a faculty member is expected to do in classes and research. For the rank and file of the faculty, their original holistic authority is now divided, delegated, and significantly abrogated.

For those who undertake leadership in the development of the university, these divisions of responsibility have their consequences. An example will illustrate: A new building makes possible added space in order that a given instructional area may round out its program for its major students. The office of space utilization, wanting to do its part in developing the university's program, allocates the necessary space. The business office, seeing that space is possible and also wanting to do its part, grants the necessary funds for requisite new equipment. The council on instruction then receives from the department its request for the new courses which the space and equipment now make possible. The council, acting from its perspective and with its portion of power, denies the request. The actions of the business office and the office of space utilization are thus nullified. Their administrators, taking forward steps in the light of their portion of perspective and power, have done useless work; so also have the department chairman and his faculty.

One might observe that this situation could have been avoided had there been "better management," i.e., had the department cleared with the council first. The catch is that the council, had it been favorable to the new courses, would not have approved them without evidence that space and equipment were available to teach the courses properly. Practically, it makes little difference which one of the various parts of the power structure one touches first; in the end, the full complement is necessary. Any one part can deny and negate the rest. Parts of the whole continually do so.

In this circumstance, it is remarkable that universities get on as well as they do. The fact that this is possible is a tribute to the operational capability of those in administrative and faculty leadership roles. These men are to be commended for their personal strength, their self-sacrificing devotion to the institutional game, their willingness to give unending hours of personal time to patching up, bridging over, and preventing from happening what otherwise is built into the system to happen.

And yet one wonders. The success of these men in preventing institutional failures may be the main factor in blinding the university community to its true situation. Members of the faculty are already eager to believe that the university is all right as it is because they are already giving their professional lives to its activities. To see the university as self-defeating is close to seeing oneself as, *ipso facto,* defeated too. This is an uncomfortable thought; a shield from the truth is useful; capable officeholders provide that shield. Faculty members can continue in their unexamined world without asking the critical questions, and the officeholders can use faculty blindness to support their own. Two layers of blindness are easier to support in the top echelons if the faculty provides one at the bottom. The natural inclination of all members of the official family of the university community is not to see the reality of the institutional situation.

Yet the reality is that cultural changes have produced a progressive division of power and responsibility within the university which culminates in a condition in which no one can take positive leadership.

PROPOSITIONS RELATING TO THE LEADERSHIP SITUATION

PROPOSITION 9

Neither faculty men nor administrators now feel that they can take leadership command.

The rank and file of the faculty feel that they cannot assume leadership because they do not own enough of the total complex of the community to make their efforts significantly effective. Administrators feel that they cannot take command for the same reason plus another reason—i.e., that it is the faculty and not the administrators to whom tradition has granted ultimate authority to shape the institution's basic affairs. Administrators can take responsibility for the management of enterprises already agreed upon in the university community, but they cannot presume to take the prerogatives of final academic authority.

Further debilitating the capacity to act on the part of either the administrator or faculty member is the latent attitude that even if a man were somehow to acquire full leadership power, he would not really know what to do with it. The ramifications of significant decisions in the total complexity of the university community are too broad and entangled for any one man to intellectually comprehend. Without significant intellectual command, confident social command is not possible either. The safer alternative is to retreat inside the limits of which one can be sure—i.e., for the faculty man to retreat to the confines of his classroom teaching and project research, and for the administrator to retreat to the management of activities clearly accepted as inside his established official domain.

PROPOSITION 10

With shrinkage in sense of command, there is shrinkage also in sense of ego, leading to resentment and a split between faculty and administration.

Faculty members, nourishing themselves on inherited visions of the pastoral campus in which the professor's way of life was the dominant pattern and the professor the dominant figure, find their loss of command a hurtful loss of ego. Resentment, easily nourished, searches for a target. Serving this purpose admirably are the administrators, who, increasing in numbers, become ready symbols for competencies now required which the professor does not himself now possess—and symbols, too, of outside pressures which seem constantly to be forcing their way into the traditional domain, over which the professor had thought himself entitled to full command. Administrators, viewing themselves primarily as agents serving the cause of the academic man, have the right to expect from professors, not resentment, but expressions of gratitude for services rendered in behalf of the academic cause; receiving few such expressions and often meeting evasiveness and subtle resistance instead, administrators can easily return the barely disguised resentment which they sense in the faculty with observations of their own concerning those in the ranks who project blame on administrators while themselves dragging their feet, protecting their personal interests, and failing to meet the conditions of the real world. A psychological wedge is driven between faculty and administration.

PROPOSITION 11

The split between faculty and administration is complicated by other cross-splittings.

If the split between faculty and administration were consistent and uniform, one could work on the problem by direct attack. But there are further complications as administrators for university services confront administrators for the colleges and departments, as administrators for a college or department confront administrators of other colleges or departments, as faculty subgroups responsible for the instructional function confront faculty subgroups responsible for the research function, as faculty subgroups responsible for undergraduate work confront faculty subgroups responsible for graduate work, and so forth. In day-to-day situations, lines of loyalty are not simple or clear. Allegiances realign themselves in diverse ways as diverse issues and problems arise.

PROPOSITION 12

A psychology of management takes over; leadership is choked out.

A would-be leader, conscientious, able, and devoted, can find himself fully occupied in adjusting himself to the constant flow of realignments as various forces inside the university recompose the vectors and valences affecting choice. Keeping in position for effective choice becomes a goal. Management ideals subtly but effectively replace leadership ideals as men give up the struggle with the complexity and ambiguity of the whole for the safer confines of a partial, already accepted, and specific office function.

For the would-be leader who finds himself cast in the role of manager of particular operations, there are seductive compensations. Though he has had to give up his dreams of positive leadership in the university as a whole, he finds he has great negative power; this is recompense. Though he can't lead the university in any comprehensive way by himself, he can stop what others start. The success of the whole depends on his willingness and ability to contribute *his* part. The institution can't move far without him. Even if he lacks power to create, he wields power to prevent or destroy. He can remind other functionaries in the system that the success of their schemes requires his participation. He can enter and withdraw from coalitions. He can add to his power by further specializing the functions inside his office operations, each new strand of operation making for a wider range of control of the whole, since each strand is a negative power, without which the rest cannot function. Newly identified operations also offer opportunity for hiring new personnel. These are the familiar temptations and tendencies present in bureaucracy, present also in the modern large university.

PROPOSITION 13

Amid these institutional and cultural complexities, the faculty confronts the future with uneasiness; their mood quickly turns to irritation in the face of any new threats to present or traditional claims.

Confronting obvious pressures for a still larger and still more complex university, the faculty senses still further loss of command, ambiguity of choice, and expansion of an intruding managerial class. What they have lost, as measured against their dreams of academic life, impresses professors more than what might be gained, as measured against the potentialities of the future. Confronted with proposals for change, they are sharply conservative, whether the proposals be for changes in the curriculum, in the form of university organization, or in designs for the future campus.

When assembled in groups where their feelings can gain by contagion, their attitude toward students can approach punitive proportions in jacking up grading standards, tightening course requirements, and raising entrance barriers. Over these matters, the academic man can claim incontestable authority because the handling of students in classes is his business and no one else's. Under conditions where enrollments bid fair to be significantly greater than resources can accommodate and the public is forced to know it, the academic man is in a position, new to him in many universities, of being able to meet pressure from outside with an equal or greater pressure from inside. *This* time, he can make the *public* change while *he* sets the conditions. This position of power feels good, oh so good, as it does to any marginal cultural group newly arrived in a position of dominance. Considerable resentment is stored up in academic men; and using the most direct route for exercising their authority, they are tempted to vent it through tightened standards on the students.

Expression of resentment can take other routes too. Should questions of policy come up in connection with the control of athletics, the faculty is prompt to name itself as ruler over these issues, defying plebeians outside the cloisters to intrude their claims on athletics in the institution. When neither students nor obvious outsiders are available as targets, the faculty will turn on its own membership, seeking those who are involved in the newer enterprises of research and service which do not fit easily in the traditional pattern of the teaching departments, denying to these men the traditional ranks and titles of the professor unless they are invited by the teaching department to membership there. Thus, commanding status and control by the present majority is guaranteed against the frightening and prospective day when intruders from new enterprises might conceivably be sufficient in number to make good their claims to the university as their rightful home, too.

PROPOSITION 14

Ever wary of administrators, the faculty guards against administrative initiative by asserting their power in councils at the top echelons of authority.

Gaining power by delegation directly from the ranks of the faculty, the councils effectively by-pass line administrators in dealing with the most important questions. The line administrators represent power intruding from outside the system, powers of denial and affirmation on budget, and powers for making commitment to outside forces which may change the obligations of professors in the system without their initiative or consent. The faculty would rather trust delegated groups of their own kind, even though they may not know these individuals personally, than trust their administrators who are known to them personally, who are constantly on duty, and who would seem, on many grounds, to be men from whom they could expect trustworthy and intelligent leadership.

The power of these councils is complete: legislative in that they form policies and principles, judicial in that they judge the acceptability or non-acceptability of specific cases (courses in the curriculum, projects in research, and so forth), executive in that they instruct their administrators what to do in carrying out their actions. Insofar as line administrators enter the process, they are perceived as entitled to do so only in their role of agent for the faculty group with whom they work. This is true not only for department chairmen at the lowest echelon, but also for vice-presidents serving as chairmen of the subcouncils (instruction, research, and so forth), who are perceived by the faculty as administrative agents for carrying out the will of these councils. In the case of the faculty council at the very top, the president, as chairman, is also perceived by the faculty as administrative agent for that group.

PROPOSITION 15

The tendency of the councils and the administrators serving them is not to act.

The obvious course of political wisdom is for an administrator who is perceived as serving the interests of a council to make it clear that he honors and serves the interests of the faculty. An administrator who not only makes this clear but who goes further to summon up an appeal to the sense of loss of the faculty, its frustrations and insecurity, can become a powerful figure, the symbol of the faculty's man. He can remain safely in this role by channeling decisions to the faculty group with which he works, being always careful to make plain that it is the group and not he that carries the power and responsibility.

The fact that decisions pile up in bunches, unmade, is hardly noticed by the administrator or the faculty as long as a feeling of identity in mutual involvement is maintained. For an administrator whose temperament leads him to behave in this fashion, decisions are likely to be difficult since they often mean that some faculty members are likely to be hurt by many of the necessary choices; no faculty member should be hurt if it can be avoided and it can often be avoided by failing to act on the problem. Administrative indecision and inaction thereby become readily sanctified as part of the pattern, sustained by emotional ties to the faculty.

PROPOSITION 16

What administrators cannot do through work with
their councils they cannot do "down the line" either.

Since authority of the line administrator has been by-passed in the delegation of faculty power to the councils on important questions, only management of what is already accepted as within the practice of the institution is left to the line administrator. This is evident when the president assembles his deans in an administrative council, or when the deans assemble their department chairmen in their executive committees; these bodies turn out to be assemblies of men primarily concerned with specific problems of making the institution run. Reviews of their minutes will reveal their problems to be the handling of such matters as the academic calendar, filling classes with necessary teachers, providing necessary equipment and housing, controlling student traffic through the curriculum, and the building of budget, as requisites to the continued and smooth operation of the university.

PROPOSITION 17

Administrators, frustrated and seeking an outlet, turn
to the companionship of their office staffs and to the

occasional use of their power over budget, but without significant effect in the leadership role.

Without a sense of progress in work with faculty councils, administrators turn easily to the formation of "councils" of their own—i.e., the members of their own office staffs, where the administrator's authority *is* direct and where there can be the comfort of a common recognition of common frustrations. Office staff meetings can benefit the management of the office and its divisions, but they offer no solution for problems which require give and take through the line with the faculty. Seductively comfortable, they offer a constant temptation to the administrator to give up his struggle to assume university leadership and to settle for managing his office.

When feeling the pain of frustration, the president and deans may occasionally exert considerable effort to make their power for development and change felt through the use of the budget. The budget is the line administrator's carrot and whip. But without related control also of the curriculum, personnel selection, promotion, and general institutional policy, such efforts at the level of mountains usually produce results at the level of molehills. An administrator who uses manipulation of money as means to the manipulation of faculty soon finds himself facing the deepest of resistance. He has violated the code of the academic man. He is much better off to avoid all appearance of manipulating the budget to manipulate men; the better out is to make quite clear to the faculty that he had no choice in budget; he has merely met the necessities of obvious demands, working by formulae and following precedent.

CONCLUSION

All these conditions produce the net effect that no one has the power to take positive leadership in the development of the university as an integral enterprise—not the line administrator, his staff, the faculty councils, the departments, or the colleges. Such power as any individual or group possesses is functionally negative with respect to the whole, fully effective only in denial of what others may try, destructive of initiative and integration, self-propelling into further snarls and splits, productive of deeper paralysis.

A man who would lead in the development of the university as an integral enterprise must meet an impossible situation. He cannot take an official position and *be* a leader. The system, as given, will not permit it.

If, in your perspective, you see positive leadership to be possible and present and adequate, then where does it show? In what circumstances? In what men?

14

TO DISENTHRALL OURSELVES

Edward Joseph Shoben, Jr.

Edward Joseph Shoben, Jr., edits the *Educational Record* and is
Director of the Commission on Academic Affairs of the American
Council on Education. Previously, he was Director of the Center for
Research and Training in Higher Education at the University of Cincin-
nati, held a variety of academic and administrative posts at Teachers
College, Columbia University, and directed the Student Counseling
Office at the State University of Iowa. His books include *The Psy-
chology of Adjustment* (with L. F. Shaffer) and *Perspectives in Psy-
chology*.

The crisis was more dramatic, noisier, more immediately concerned with danger and death. But for those who
believe with H. G. Wells that civilization is indeed a race
between education and catastrophe, it was no more important;
and for those who take seriously the crises of our own time,
Lincoln's words retain their urgency. In December of 1862, in
the depths of the Civil War's dark brutalities, he prepared a
message for the Congress, saying: "The dogmas of the quiet
past are inadequate to the stormy present . . . . As our case is
new, we must think anew, act anew. We must disenthrall
ourselves. . . ."

Addressed to the official personnel of our colleges and universities a century later, that admonition to "disenthrall ourselves"
may meet with some resistance, but no recommendation is more
apt. The resistance stems, understandably if only partially, from
the fact that today's professors and administrators are people
who have known a great depression and history's most harrow-
ing war, yet seen the nation and its institutions, including its

institutions of higher learning, not only survive but reach new levels of world leadership and domestic affluence. Theirs has hardly been a quiet past; and while they are unlikely to deny the present's storminess, they must still on occasion acknowledge its very tangible advantages. Disenthrall ourselves from *what*, for heaven's sake? Where is the relevance of Lincoln's visionary words for the busy academics of this last third of the twentieth century?

The answer lies in four realities that, taken together, define a radically transformed world and an equally radically revised role for colleges and universities. It is for this reason—because our case is new—that we must think anew, act anew.

THE TEMPO OF CHANGE

The first of these four realities is the tempo of social change. So much has been said about this aspect of contemporary culture that it is hard to discuss it without clichés, but its pervasive and revolutionary force is not lessened by the banalities of our language. The primary facts are familiar ones and require only brief reminders here.

In the past 25 years, we have not only turned the energy of the atom into a potentially genocidal weapon, begun with high success the exploration of space, and stepped over the threshold of industrial automation. We have also been brought face to face with a variety of entirely novel social probabilities. The accessibility of inexpensive oral contraceptives implies a marked and rapid revision of our codes of sexual conduct and the ideological and psychological bases on which they have found their credibility. The impact on marriage as an institution is not easy to predict. Our technology of communication and transportation, largely a product of the past quarter-century, has tied the nations of the world into a system of interdependence that properly makes events in once exotic places like Cambodia or the Congo matters of great concern in New York and Dallas; and mountains, deserts, and oceans have become essentially irrelevant as guarantees of a state's security, autonomy, or importance. The rejection of colonialism has been timed in general to the rejection by Negroes in the United States of second-class citizenship, and the long Caucasian hegemony in both domestic and international spheres is under a threat which, in many quarters, entails special agonies and nerve-wracking complexities. If the industrial application of computers and servomechanisms means freedom from undignified toil and opens new vistas of comfortable leisure, it also raises the troubling question of where men are to find new and viable sources of pride and self-esteem when the ancient Western ethic of work loses its vitality.

After all, this familiar but deeply revolutionary catalogue must be capped with some brief attention to the thoughtways that both underlie and are a consequence of our booming technology and its social reverberations. There is not yet a widely accepted single name for these intellectual processes, but they are concerned primarily with the design and management of large-scale systems.[1] They permeate econometrics and modern control theory, are the basis of the programming and use of big computers, pervade management science and the field of operations research, and enter into the strategic as well as the technological issues connected with weapons systems. Whatever their assets—and they are obviously manifold—these systems-oriented approaches to contemporary problems begin not with a concern for persons, but with a search for predictability, reliability, and efficiency. Such a quest leads, as a by-product at least, to a low premium on the individual human being; and to the extent that it is in some sense successful, it subtly alters our ways of thinking about ourselves, our fellows, and the human condition. Nudged by the very real contributions of the systems scientists and computer engineers, we tend a little more to evaluate men as systemic units. Sheer efficiency becomes the touchstone of personal judgment, and if men fall below some minimally acceptable standard of efficiency, the central question becomes one of whether it is more economic to repair them (often psychiatrically) or to replace them. Thus, the revolution of our time has far more in common with the revolutions associated with the ideas of Galileo and Darwin than with those associated with changes in the manufacture and distribution of artifacts; ours is a revolution in man's image of himself, in the very way that we conceive ourselves and our relationships to each other.

TRADITIONS IN EXTREMIS

Educationally, the implications here are clear. Because our society is in process of radical transformation at an unprecedented rate, the past is no longer a sufficient guide to the future. For this reason, the traditional function of the undergraduate college—the transmitting of the cultural heritage to young people destined for some form of social leadership—is simply inadequate. It is not that the great human legacy has lost its value. Indeed, now as never before, one can make a strong case for the importance of our connections with the past and for the humanizing merits of developing an informed sense among students of membership in the long, proud pageant of man. But when yesterday no longer forecasts the nature of tomorrow, when the experience of sons is so startlingly different from the experience of fathers, then the enterprise of education must find new sources of vitality and relevance.

In the curriculum, this state of affairs demands not only a presentation of our cultural inheritance and of what is now known. It makes necessary a winnowing of our inherited knowledge in the light of the uncertainties of the future and the urgent problems of the present. Our traditions, in short, must be subject to responsible and intensive criticism. And if teaching is to be effective, it must embrace not only scholarly thoroughness and clarity, but also a demonstration of responsible criticism. One can argue that if scholarship itself is to be more than antiquarianism, a methodological exercise, or a harnessing of intellect to technology, then it must prove its value as a basis for this kind of critical and functionally humane perspective on the sources of our culture. Teaching students "to think" has long been an academic piety; it is now a necessity that must be faced and met in the most hardheaded fashion if colleges and universities are to remain the great agents of civilization that they have historically been. Ready-made answers are not available, but it seems only the blunt truth that institutions which fail to address themselves systematically to this problem are simply irresponsible.

NOVELTY OF NUMBERS

Our second reality is that of numbers. Here again the story is superficially familiar. We all know that there are currently about 6.5 million students roaming our halls of higher learning. In 1940, the comparable figure approximated 1.5 million. In that year, the percentage of college-age youth actually enrolled was 14. In the mid-1960's, that percentage came close to 48. By 1975, we can anticipate total student enrollments of roughly nine million or something in excess of 60 per cent of youngsters between the ages of 17 and 21. The problems of housing such rapidly increasing numbers, providing parking spaces for their cars, and recruiting faculty members to meet their classes are much too close to require underscoring.

Two points, however, may not be quite so apparent. A little surprisingly, the leaping increments in college attendance have also produced an increase in overall quality. In part, this upgrading in student competence may be attributed to the improved instruction in elementary and secondary schools, particularly in the last decade. It is easy to demonstrate that today's freshmen come to college with both a wider range of information and a superior mastery of mathematics, English, and modern foreign languages than was true, on the average, of their parents a scant generation ago. More importantly, rising enrollments have meant rising opportunities for the most able youngsters. A generation ago, only about half of the brightest high school graduates—those in the top fifteen per cent of the population in measured intelligence—continued their formal education. In 1965, over two-thirds of the students in that bracket of ability went on to college. If we take high school achievement as our index, we note that in 1940 appreciably less than half of the youngsters ranking in the upper fifty per cent of their high school graduating classes went on to college; today that figure has passed the seventy per cent mark. In short, as our colleges and universities have absorbed more students, they have also absorbed more talented ones at a higher level of pre-college training. So far then, the burgeoning of numbers has meant an accompanying growth in intellectual quality.

Nevertheless, the second point to be made here remains crucial. Increases in absolute numbers of students and in proportions of college-age youth in the growing population inevitably mean increases in the diversity of college student bodies. Not only must our institutions cope educatively with more youngsters, but with more *kinds* of youngsters. This inexorable fact of growing diversity raises the question of whether we mean it when we give voice to certain of our humane aspirations and to some of our national goals. An example, important both for its source and for the way in which it echoes widely shared sentiments, comes from the platform of the Democratic Party in 1964:

> Our task is to make the national purpose serve the human purpose: that every person shall have the opportunity to become all that he or she is capable of becoming.
>
> We believe that knowledge is essential to individual freedom and to the conduct of free society. We believe that education is the surest and most profitable investment a nation can make.
>
> Regardless of family financial status, therefore, education should be open to every boy or girl in America up to the highest level which he or she is able to master.

Regardless of political preferences, there are few among us who would dissent from such an aim. Yet it poses questions as fraught with poignancy as with technical difficulties: What are the highest levels of education which various groups within our population are able to master? How can we tell? And what are our resources for appropriate action?

DIVERSITY'S MEANING

Up to now, we have been able to avoid these worrisome queries while cherishing our ambitions. It has been a long time since we quarreled with each other about whether elementary education should be universal. There is still room for doubts about secondary education, but we have reached a high degree of agreement *by supporting an increasing diversity in high school programs* as well as by appealing to such collateral matters as keeping youngsters of high school age out of the labor market. We are now coming rapidly to the moment of decision when we must find some way, at once rational and humane, to balance the standards of higher education with the huge spectrum of abilities over which American youth is distributed. Conceivably, we could solve (as seems probable) the financial problems of college attendance only to find ourselves developing exclusionary policies of admission on the grounds of some straightforward concept of stupidity. Given the still unresolved issues bound up with the nature of intelligence, and given the ambiguous character of academic grades (see pp. 125–135), we are liable to some disquieting uncertainties and some distressing feelings of guilt if we move too rapidly toward a control of enrollments on such a basis. Like the Queries of the Quakers, this matter may be one less to be settled than to be thought about vigorously and seriously. Unhappily, there is little evidence that many of our colleges and universities are facing up to this close-at-hand difficulty in any systematic fashion.

In any event, diversity of background, ability, and drive is almost sure to be the hallmark of most American student bodies in the very near future if such is not already the case. The breadth of these differences makes it highly improbable that a homogeneous curriculum, traditional methods of teaching, or the customary allotments of time in either credit-hours or terms will serve equally well the diverse elements within institutional enrollments. *De facto* equality of educational opportunity demands attention to the varying rates at which diverse students learn, their frequently quite different styles of learning, and their divergent motivations and personal orientations. We already know that the lecture, the conventional preference among modes of college instruction, is an inefficient and expensive means of promoting learning per unit cost. In the light of the numbers and diversity of students with which we must contend now and in the years ahead, we are doomed to produce far less than optimum learning, just as we are doomed to provide far less than truly equal opportunities for large segments of our college-going youth, if we continue our now modal patterns of teaching and of organizing the learning experiences that define our curricula. Once again, because our case is new, we must think anew.

THE DEMAND FOR RELEVANCE

From the tempo of social change and the increase in student bodies, it is easy to infer—and to find ample confirmation in recent events—the third of our transforming realities: a new and more urgently presented set of demands by students on their educational experience. Protests and demonstrations on a variety of campuses are the most public and dramatic symptom of this component in the radically altered *Zeitgeist* of academia, but their meaning is not given by either their intensity or their immediate causes. Student riots are hardly novelties—witness the heated cannon balls rolled down the corridors at Hobart in 1811, the "bell and shooting" by which Georgia students celebrated Christmas Eve in 1824, or the more recent panty raids of the 1950's. The novelty in the modern student temper lies essentially in a tripartite emphasis on more generous human relationships, on social criticism, and on educational relevance. And the greatest of these is relevance.

When one strips away the irresponsible hotheadedness, the disposition to adolescent hi jinks, and a tendency simply to run with the crowd—all of which are certainly present—one finds an impressive reflection in student attitudes of the forces at work in our larger society.[2] Predominant themes include the subtle processes of dehumanization, symbolized by the IBM card; a distrust of the world which youth has inherited from its elders, the emblems of which are atomic weaponry and such military involvements as those in Viet Nam and Santo Domingo; and the disarticulation of the intellectual life from the direct application of human ideals like love and justice in the community, a concern represented by students' leaving their classrooms to join the Peace Corps or to participate in the civil rights movement. While the proportion of actual activists among undergraduates is undoubtedly low, this group is important in two ways. By and

large, these students are among the highest in both academic
ability and academic achievement on their campuses; and they
heavily influence the tone of their institutions even where demonstrations and protest meetings are few or nonexistent. The
college or university that is inattentive, in its curriculum and in
its instructional effort, to this element invites both trouble and a
kind of functional extinction.

Nor are the issues substantively very different if the student
mood in a particular place is one of apathy. By the criterion of
sheer numbers, apathy remains the predominant undergraduate
temper, and there are far more students whose educative growth
demands a constructive awakening than those whose verve
needs curbing. The central point here, however, is that apathy
frequently is a manifestation of passive resistance to an unsatis-
fying or frustrating situation; and a lack of commitment to
college can and often does imply a lack of anything perceived as
worthy of commitment. Standards of worthiness may properly
vary markedly between students and faculty, and student standards are by no means necessarily the most appropriate ones.
Nevertheless, a condition necessary for the business of education to proceed effectively is an institutional ambience in which
such differences can be openly and fairly considered and in
which undergraduate views are accorded genuine respect.

VALUES OF THE DISCONTENTED

The reasons for such respect are many, but a central one is
that the current generation is struggling to make articulate in
modern terms the very values that have been most cherished in
the history of liberal education. Concern about one's fellows, an
informed involvement in the affairs of citizenship, and a strongly
interiorized sense of love and justice have long animated the
educational adventure; and whatever their shortcomings, their
immaturities, or their impatience with very authentic complexities, today's youngsters are searching—and asking for help in
their quest—for ways to develop just such qualities.

Their objection, for example, to the hoary doctrine of *in loco
parentis* is grounded in the conviction that good parents are
facilitative as well as restrictive, are lovingly concerned person-

ally with their offspring as well as insistent on the abstract rules of household and community. Because there are few colleges that now can play (if they ever could) the positive, personalized, and developmental role of a parent, the students argue that institutions can only hypocritically claim the status of surrogate parents as the basis for their laying down and enforcing restrictive regulations. It is not the function of parenthood that is being exercised; it is the function of a self-perpetuating and self-protective bureaucracy. Thus, such trivia as dormitory hours and rules affecting men's and women's visiting each other in residence halls become important not in themselves but for what they symbolize; and what they symbolize to the young people involved is not a genuine and appropriate interest in their own moral development but a way of avoiding possibly embarrassing publicity and the risk of disfavor among legislators or trustees. Most of all, the *in loco parentis* doctrine is discontinuous with the ethos of our time and irrelevant to the norms of the larger society. The life demanded by it is an unnecessarily more restricted one than the life that can be lived off campus, and it is hard to find any convincing *educational* reason for the penalties that students must pay simply because they are students.

Such illustrations can be readily multiplied. Their point, of course, is not to demonstrate that students are inevitably or even most frequently right, but that their attitudes stem from concerns that the proponents of the liberal arts can only applaud and from a sense of a troubled disharmony between the world of the campus and the world beyond its boundaries as they experience it. Not only do the rules of conduct within the college appear badly out of phase with the rules outside; the curriculum and the patterns of instruction seem sharply removed from the life of the larger society. Many students report that they learn far more that fits them for citizenship on picket lines, in VISTA or the Peace Corps, or in the civil rights movement than they do in classrooms, and that the popularity of work-study programs derives in part from the dullness and the lack of cogency in study in relation to the authenticity of the work experience. The significance of these views is that they make articulate the discontent of large numbers. While they may be fumbling in

their approach and sometimes murky in their ideas, today's
students—brighter and better informed than any previous generation to walk our college corridors—are eager to learn how to
think productively about the world they live in and to find in
their professors models of the cultivated mind at work on the
crucial problems of men. If their disappointment can be somehow explained, it cannot be explained away; and the primary
question posed by their demand for relevance in their educational experience is that of whether a particular college or
university can examine itself squarely and conclude either that
the demand is inappropriate or that it is being met. Just as the
challenge applies to institutions, so it applies, too, to individual
faculty members.

THE FACULTY AND ITS ROLES

There is little doubt that the faculty of a college defines both
its spirit and its spheres and levels of effectiveness. There is
equally little doubt that a faculty is composed of individuals on
whose academic competence an institution's educational and
scholarly productivity depends. But a faculty is also a collectivity, organized in a fashion that impedes or facilitates its work
What is its work?

Oddly enough, the catalogue of professorial tasks is not a
small one. Over time, the college instructor has been called upon
to extend the frontiers of human knowledge, to resynthesize and
reinterpret knowledge, to impart significant information and
ideas to young people, to provide a good example of conduct for
youth and to indoctrinate the young in the moral (and sometimes the religious) traditions of their culture, to furnish personal counsel to students, to play a part in the determination of
policy and in the management of his department and occasionally in his institution, to render various forms of intellectually
based public service, to represent the professional concerns of
his special discipline to his institution and to the public at large,
and many more. Obviously, these functions have never been
equally weighted, and some of them have waxed over history
while others have waned. The point, however, is that a professor

plays many roles and occupies a deceptively complex niche in the hall of the professions.

HYPOTHESIS OF DIVISION

An analysis of recent trends in the activities of faculty members gives rise to the strong hypothesis that those tasks which bring professors and students into closest relationship have been progressively less rewarded and therefore weaker, whereas those which separate professors from students have been progressively more rewarded and therefore more definitive of the actual work of faculties. The result has been a degree of alienation between students and their mentors and the perceived irrelevance in their educational experience of which so many undergraduates complain.

For example, as the extent of religious control over colleges and universities declined, there was a concomitant decline in the character-building objective once so vital in American higher education. With secularization a dominant motif in the larger society, the professorial functions of moral indoctrination and personal counseling fell away for sheer want of support in the culture at large. In a specialized and secularized way, they have been taken over by specialists in student personnel work and the clinical professions, oriented much more toward the resolving of such human problems as emotional upset, troubled interpersonal relations, difficulties in the planning of careers, or actual mental illness than toward the development of character. Under this sort of division of labor, emphases in the curriculum and in instructional patterns on the significance of subject matter for characterological growth or decisions about one's conduct have also fallen away. In consequence, classrooms have been cleared of a certain stuffiness and an atmosphere of frequent preachment; but there has also been a lessened sense of faculty responsibility for students as persons, and a compelling justification has at least been put ready to hand for a lessened interest in the personal concerns of undergraduates as developing human beings. These tendencies have been reinforced, of course, by the sheer force of hugely increased numbers.

On the other hand, three quite different trends have increasingly moved professors into a predominantly scholarly role in which their primary audience is their disciplinary colleagues rather than their students or the official personnel of their institutions. One is the establishment of the Ph.D. as the faculty union card. A German import, the degree originally stood witness to advanced scholarship in primarily the natural sciences. Very rapidly, however, it became the hallmark of respectability in all departments of knowledge, and its special stress on research attainments somehow generalized to become also the basic qualification for teaching, too. This development is understandable in the light of an essentially simultaneous increase in the centrality of research and publication as the criteria of professional success and the routes to promotions and salary increments. In 1958, Caplow and McGee demonstrated that research and publication were very often the only bases on which employment in a college or university was granted or withheld and quite frequently the only grounds for decisions about a professor's advancement.[3] There is no evidence to suggest any significant change in this pattern. With respect to both the quickly developed vitality of the Ph.D. and the greatly increased emphasis on research, the rise of science in Western culture through the last half of the nineteenth and the twentieth centuries was no doubt crucial.

The rise of science also was highly relevant to our third trend, the growth of professional associations. Rare is the professor who does not belong to at least one of the societies into which his discipline is *organized* or who does not look forward to its published journals, its annual meetings, its special services to members, and the contributions of its committees. His identity pivots in large part on his acceptance by the Modern Language Association or the American Chemical Society and on the status he commands among his fellow members. As a result, he is subject to a conflict of loyalties between his discipline, represented by its society, which determines in high degree his reputation and his self-concept, and his institution, which pays his salary and gives him a place in which to work. This situation has been enormously elaborated as the professional societies, responding to the growth of knowledge, have undergone various forms of mitosis to make room for new specialties, concerned with increasingly narrower and more intensive brands of investigation and scholarship. Inevitably, a divisive influence has been exercised, reshaping the faculty member's image of himself and the perceived role he plays in the public eye. No longer is he the sage, reflective, and broadly cultivated man whose wise judgments can properly be sought over a wide range of issues; rather, he is known by the distinctiveness of that fractional part of his discipline in which he has developed superior expertise.

Taken together, these three tendencies—the rise of the Ph.D., the centrality of research and publication, and the growth of professional societies—have determined conditions under which a professor's identity, reputation, rank, and salary are much more dependent on what he does in his study or his laboratory than in his classroom. Indeed, students can be a real distraction from the productive functions according to which success is defined. Again, the effect has been to enlarge, sometimes subtly and sometimes blatantly, the degree of alienation between faculty and student body.

Finally, the demand for expert brainpower, particularly since World War II but as a necessity in a highly technologized society, has given a new impetus to the public service functions of the professoriate. If philosophers have not yet become kings, faculty members have certainly come into their own. Opportunities to serve government agencies and industrial organizations in consultative capacities are available with considerable and growing frequency, and posts to be filled in business or government during leaves of absence or sabbatical years are not uncommon. Performing these functions is not only pleasantly lucrative; it makes possible contributions to society of genuine importance, and potentially at least, it brings the perspectives of academic life and the immediacies of the outside world into a closer and more harmonious relationship. But because it is not easy to involve students in meaningful ways in such enterprises, the enlargement of the public service function has tended to deepen the rift between multi-occupied professors and the youngsters who come to them in search of a relevant education. The problem, of course, is one of how to make more accessible to youth the experience of men who have learned to move with relative ease between the ivory tower, with its long view of the human condition, and the world of practical affairs, with its realistic hurly-burly and harshly direct responsibilities.

In any case, the first step in dealing with the educational consequences of this diffusion of faculty commitments may be deliberately to narrow the gap between a student's expectancies and his fulfillment. The abstract and pious promises of institutional catalogues, with their talk of preparation for citizenship and the development of the whole person, seldom mirror the realities that an undergraduate encounters on his arrival at the campus; and there is at least room to believe that this abridgment of an implied contract is significantly perceived as both a frustration of a youngster's educational quest and a sign that he and his development occupy low priorities in the actual conduct of the college.

The accusation and the challenge here point directly at faculties—*not* administrators—who typically control in an iron-fisted way the processes of instruction, evaluation, and curricular development at their institutions. If learning is to be the authentic basis for an academic community, then professors must take the lead and drastically re-examine their role in making it so.

A SUMMARIZING CODA

Thus we are brought back to the circumstances to which Lincoln's admonition to disenthrall ourselves seems a necessary first response. If our colleges and universities are to fulfill their vital mission as educational agencies in an age when education is literally the nation's (and perhaps the world's) most important resource, they must radically rethink the conditions under which they operate and the legitimate options open to them. This task of reconceiving the nature of higher education does not lack precedents; every age must review its inherited modes of reaction if it is to be a lively and viable one. In our era, the job differs only in its complexity and its singular urgency.

The complexity and urgency are indicated in large part by the four realities that have been discussed here. First of all, the social context in which higher education moves and has its being is marked by a rapidity of change never known before. While the process of change produces high advantages, it also seriously strains the threads of human continuity, making tomorrow improbable of understanding on the basis of yesterday's experience. Educationally, this state of affairs means that the sheer transmission of the cultural heritage—the accumulated experience of all our yesterdays—is no longer sufficient, however necessary it may be, as the core of a modern man's education. Second, our efforts to meet the curricular and instructional requirements imposed by the tempo of social change are complicated not only by new numbers of students, but by a new diversity in their backgrounds, abilities, and aspirations. The vision of universal higher education has flashed across our mind's eye, and in general, we have found it good. But to realize that dream, we must invent programs and procedures that have heretofore never been thought of. The legacy of elitist educational practices is unlikely to be the best or even the relevant equipment for the great many whom our colleges and universities must serve. Third, the new generation of students comprises children of the modern world of whirling change. Rather brighter and clearly better informed than their predecessors, they are demanding an education that helps them not only to survive but to live with zest and meaning in that world. The curricular offerings and the instructional practices that were suitable for yesterday's classrooms are, in the eyes of those who occupy those lecture halls today, simply too lacking in demonstrable cogency. And finally, as history has reshaped the highly varied roles of the professoriate, it has tended to strengthen those faculty functions which entail cleavages between instructors and students and to weaken those which bring the two groups together. At the same time, some of their strongly reinforced activities provide an opportunity for faculty members to enrich the educational climate of their campuses and to furnish students with access to a broader range of educative experience than ever before.

If our problems are sizeable, none is insuperable. The first condition for their resolution, however, is that we disenthrall ourselves—from the policies and practices of a stabler day, from the memories of smallness and homogeneity in our student bodies, from a curriculum and from ways of instruction and campus management which are out of phase with the world of today's students, and from a certain blindness in our awareness and balancing of the diverse roles of professors. Once Lincoln's admonition has been met, we will have taken a long stride toward developing a productive partnership in learning between our students and our faculties.

NOTES

1. R. Boguslaw, *The New Utopians* (Englewood Cliffs, N. J.: Prentice-Hall, 1966).

2. L. Dennis and J. Kauffman (eds.), *The College and the Student* (Washington, D. C.: American Council on Education, 1966); and E. J. Shoben, Jr., *Students, Stress, and the College Experience* (Washington, D. C.: United States National Student Association, 1966).

3. T. Caplow and R. J. McGee, *The Academic Marketplace* (New York: Basic Books, 1958).

BOOKS FOR
FURTHER STUDY

Association of American Colleges. *Reflections on the Role of Liberal Education.* Washington, D. C.: Association of American Colleges, 1964.

Bell, D. *The Reforming of General Education.* New York: Columbia University Press, 1966.

Bruner, J. *Toward a Theory of Instruction.* Cambridge, Mass.: Harvard University Press, 1966.

Caplow, T., and R. J. McGee. *The Academic Marketplace.* Garden City, N. Y.: Doubleday Anchor, 1965 (Basic Books, 1958).

Conant, J. *The Citadel of Learning.* New Haven: Yale University Press, 1956.

Dennis, L. E., and J. F. Kauffman (eds.). *The College and the Student.* Washington: American Council on Education, 1966.

Keniston, K. *The Uncommitted.* New York: Harcourt, Brace, and World, 1966.

Kerr, C. *The Uses of the University.* Cambridge, Mass.: Harvard University Press, 1963.

Klotsche, J. M. *The Urban University.* New York: Harper & Row, 1966.

Lynd, R. S. *Knowledge for What?* New York: Grove Press, 1964 (Princeton, 1939).

McGrath, E. J. (ed.). *Universal Higher Education.* New York: McGraw-Hill, 1966.

Mager, R. F. *Preparing Instructional Objectives.* Palo Alto, Calif.: Fearon Publishers, 1962.

Newman, J. H. *The Idea of a University.* Garden City, N. Y.: Doubleday Image, 1959 (1852).

Perkins, J. *The University in Transition.* Princeton, N. J.: Princeton University Press, 1966.

Rudolph, F. *The American College and University: A History.* New York: Random House, 1965.

Sanford, N. (ed.). *The American College.* New York: Wiley, 1962.

Select Committee, Academic Senate. *Education at Berkeley.* Berkeley, California: University of California Press, 1966.

Shoben, E. J., Jr. *Students, Stress, and the College Experience.* Washington, D. C.: Council Press for the U. S. National Student Association, May, 1966.

Sutherland, R. L., *et al.* (eds.). *Personality Factors on the College Campus.* Austin, Texas: The Hogg Foundation for Mental Health, 1962.

Thomas, R. *The Search for a Common Learning: General Education, 1800–1960.* New York: McGraw-Hill, 1962.

Veblen, T. *The Higher Learning in America.* New York: Hill and Wang, 1962 (Huebsch, 1918).

Wilson, L. *The Academic Man: Sociology of a Profession.* New York: Oxford University Press, 1942.

ACKNOWLEDGMENTS

Paul L. Dressel and Irvin J. Lehmann, "The Impact of Higher Education on Student Attitudes, Values, and Critical Thinking Abilities," *Educational Record,* Vol. 46, No. 3 (Summer 1965), 248–58. Reprinted by permission of the American Council on Education and the authors.

Ruth E. Eckert and Daniel C. Neale, "Teachers and Teaching," *Review of Educational Research,* Vol. 35, No. 4 (1965). Reprinted by permission of the American Educational Research Association and the authors.

John W. Gardner, "The Flight from Teaching," *The Carnegie Foundation for the Advancement of Teaching, Fifty-ninth Annual Report, 1963–64,* pp. 11–22. Reprinted by permission of the Foundation and the author.

Howard E. Gruber, "The Uses and Abuses of Negative Results," originally published as "The Future of Self Directed Study," *Approach to Independent Study,* New Dimensions in Higher Education No. 13, OE-50041 (Washington: U. S. Department of Health, Education, and Welfare, 1965), pp. 1–10. Reprinted by permission of the author and Winslow R. Hatch, Director, Clearinghouse of Studies on Higher Education, Division of Higher Education, U. S. Department of Health, Education, and Welfare.

Donald P. Hoyt, "The Criterion Problem in Higher Education," *North Central News Bulletin,* Vol. 25, No. 8 (May, 1966), 3–16. Reprinted by permission of the *North Central News Bulletin* and the author.

William R. Hutchison, "Yes, John, There are Teachers on the Faculty," *The American Scholar,* Vol. 35, No. 3 (Summer, 1966), 430–41. Copyright © 1966 by the United Chapters of Phi Beta Kappa. Reprinted by permission of the publishers and the author.

Henry C. Johnson, Jr., "Are Our Universities Schools?" *Harvard*

Educational Review, Vol. 35 (1965), 165–77. Reprinted by permission of the *Harvard Educational Review* and the author.

Ross L. Mooney, "The Problem of Leadership in the University," *Harvard Educational Review,* Vol. 33 (1963), 42–57. Reprinted by permission of the *Harvard Educational Review* and the author.

C. Robert Pace, "Five College Environments," *College Board Review,* Spring, 1960. Reprinted by permission of the College Entrance Examination Board and the author.

Sidney L. Pressey, "Two Basic Neglected Psychoeducational Problems," *American Psychologist,* Vol. 20, No. 6 (June, 1965), 391–95. Reprinted by permission of the American Psychological Association and the author.

Laurence Siegel, "The Contributions and Implications of Recent Research Related to Improving Teaching and Learning," paper read at the Tennessee College Association, Memphis, March 31, 1966. Used by permission of the author.

Logan Wilson, "Setting Institutional Priorities," *Pressures and Priorities in Higher Education,* The Proceedings of the Twentieth Annual National Conference on Higher Education (Washington: Association for Higher Education, 1965), pp. 33–39. Reprinted by permission of the Association for Higher Education and the author.